RAINBOW PEOPLE

Supporting the Disabled to Become Enabled

Barbara Woodward

First Published in Australia by Aurora House
www.aurorahouse.com.au

This edition published 2017

Typesetting and Cover Design: WorkingType Studio

ISBN number: 9780987617712 (paperback)

National Library of Australia Cataloguing-in-Publication entry (paperback)

Creator: Woodward, Barbara, author.
Title: Rainbow People / Barbara Woodward.
ISBN: 9780987617712 (paperback)
Subjects: People with disabilities--Australia.
Ability.
Life skills.

I dedicate this to humanitarian Moira Theresa Kelly (A.O.) who lives as the personification of love with wings on.

My special acknowledgment to Jean Rogers, who grew in wisdom from the ashes of hurt; she was my special friend and teacher.

Foreword

Rainbow People is a collection of memories from Barbara Woodward's ambitious life of service. She writes with the professional caregiver as her prime audience, but her stories have much to offer any reader.

Barbara has worked with the disabled for more than thirty years. A welfare course was her entrance into this world, with psychology studies further supporting her work. Yet Barbara considers her clients some of her most inspiring teachers.

Rainbow People retells the twists and turns Barbara faced during her work with adults who had varying disabilities, and her experiences offer insights to the current minds and the next generation of care givers.

Barbara's clients come to life as she tells her stories, and then she leads us to rethink... "First impressions don't always tell the whole story... There is always another story." She is forever promoting a greater awareness of these multi-layered people.

We learn of Robbie and his outbursts, and many others who have spent years in the health care system. Each client presents a characteristic or feature that the reader will be able to identify with and relate to someone in their own local community.

Barbara promotes the idea that simple kindness costs

little, but it must be authentic. A small investment of genuine interest and care in our daily interactions with those less able than ourselves can have far-reaching effects for others, as well as ourselves as human beings.

Her experience has allowed insight into a world unfamiliar to many. With this knowledge, we are all empowered to adjust our mindset and be ready for our next experience with a person who has a disability challenge.

At times *Rainbow People* is a record of behaviour interventions that have had a profound influence on Barbara's clients and their families. As the author states, "May we not forget, with any form of disability, no one of us is immune." While this statement may not be our motivation to intervene in the lives of those with disability challenges, it may promote an awareness and lead to a stronger co-existence, moving towards true integration in our world.

Praise for Barbara's writings extend to her influence in my own work, where I endeavour to 'be the voice' for the children and families I work with, and support them to 'find *their* voice'. *Rainbow People* will engage and influence you in your own humanitarian journey.

Moira Kelly A.O.

"Society's accumulated myths and fears about disability... are as handicapping as are the physical limitations that flow from actual impairment"

— William J. Brennan, Jr

INTRODUCTION

All the stories in this book are true and I can recall them as if they occurred yesterday. Naturally, I have changed the names for most individuals mentioned to preserve their privacy. I have adopted the same principle for named work places. However, I felt it appropriate to name certain people whose goodness deserves my personal acknowledgment. I will use the term 'client' when referring to any disabled person I have worked with, as this is how they are formally referred to within service-based work places.

I invite you to share my journey of working within the disability field, so you can understand the influential way so many special individuals crossed my path. They offer a voice to a landscape that has often been fraught with misunderstanding and prejudice. You will meet some of these lovely people, who will ask you to listen very carefully, as they have something valuable to say about their emotional and psychological wellbeing. It is through their experiences that I offer a philosophical discourse on the relationship we may have with anyone who may seem different.

It was through a chance encounter while I was a student that I was first introduced to disability. On a chilly winter's morning, I was standing at the corner of a tired and sinister-looking building, waiting for my supervisor. Little did I know I would find myself in a most surprising and unusual predicament, which literally pushed me into the career path I was inevitably destined to pursue.

The events that followed further led me to the people and places that opened my mind and world to different possibilities and life choices. Before stumbling into that building, I had intended to be involved in the welfare justice system. However, it seemed the universe had different plans for me and my career. Having now walked that path, I can share the many profound realisations of the past thirty plus years about what my 'clients' were able to teach me along this much-travelled road. We welcome you to join us.

Before I completed the welfare officer course, I was aware of the standard range of disabilities, such as blindness, deafness, wheelchair bound, etc. My relative ignorance of more complex disabilities was simply due to not having been personally exposed to those who present such disabilities. Throughout my childhood years, I heard all the derogatory terms about those who, to me, appeared odd looking, odd sounding or behaved differently in some way. While I considered these comments cruel, my awareness did not extend to their true status and need for complete respect. I took for granted that human inequities existed on many levels but were all too complex to understand.

I invite readers to embrace this book as a source of hope and personal growth. This process can begin when I introduce you to the many unique individuals I have worked with throughout my career.

Apart from more general information about disability, I offer a broad range of specific details to help dispel much of the misinformation about what having a disability entails. I explain how in the past the two extreme views of the disabled as being either mentally incompetent or pitied/feared have only served to prevent their true integration within our society. This has resulted in, at best, their current measured coexistence within the broader population. But it is a start.

The subsequent chapters present individuals who may be considered a composite of the hundreds of others I have met along my travels. Their stories may melt your heart and move your mind to a renewed understanding of what being disabled really means — perhaps these 'intellectually disabled' people may even surprise you.

You will meet people such as Robbie, who was my inspiration for the title of this book. He will speak to you after he has created a huge emotional storm that resulted in a broken window and scattered chairs — but you will not think him a violent person. Then there's Gina who, while misunderstood on so many levels, will sweeten your thoughts about what being labelled a psychotic can mean. You will discover the simple solution found for Jodie's strange obsessive habit known as pica (consuming unsavoury substances), as well as Tim's major vacuum cleaner dilemma — both stories will sharpen your imagination. You will also meet Jane, a lady who was often feared, but as you get to know her, you will see her endearing side.

A welcomed aspect of working with the disabled is their honesty and humour. Unlike many of us, they are able to laugh at themselves and sometimes may even trust someone enough to let them know what is in their hearts; I have learnt it only takes a kind word to convey that you are in tune with their feelings. They show you when they are fearful and anxious but you may only see violence. However, they also ask you to take another look, as first impressions don't always tell the whole story. And there is *always* another story.

Unfortunately, there are those who look down on their clients. I have known carers who feel embarrassed to say they work in disability or, alternatively, feel superior in their supervisory role — neither view is worthy of their position. So, hopefully, my story will help enrich the general public's view of disabled individuals and, in particular, carers' personal sense of involvement with them, promoting a greater awareness of these multi-faceted people. My wish for you is to embrace your role positively and feel a sense of pride and purpose in your work. You may have a disabled relative and hope that he/she is considered worthy enough to be seen for who they are and deemed equal in what really matters.

This book invites readers to explore their potential prejudices, to wonder what it means to stand in someone else's shoes so they can understand them better and, in the process, learn more about themselves. There is an ongoing need for open dialogue between 'clients' and their care workers, supervisors, policymakers, fund managers, psychologists, etc. All need to be standing on the same page in practice, not just in policy, to avoid confusion or potential conflict for all concerned.

A lady who is blind and cannot speak English struggles to feel safe even in her own home, fearing someone will hit her from behind. Who would place her in such a position? Who becomes her voice? Logically, it is the people who work with her every day that have the duty to ensure she feels secure and protected. Yet even in such circumstances, egos can get in the way of common sense.

To be able to recite 'The Charter of Human Rights' does not guarantee its application in practice. It is easy to feel a false sense of achievement, leading to complacency, just by having attractive, creative posters on the walls or fancy words in folders. Our clients want the rhetoric of 'best practice' to be directly translated to them, for it is a joy to see a client have a positive outcome when staff speak out on their behalf — even if it means respectfully pushing the cause over those ego barriers.

I share how an overanxious man was finally able to feel free when staff stood up for him in the face of bullying. He assumed that he was in danger every day but was afraid to tell anyone, and having come from a large institution, he felt he had no power. He will tell you how any direct care workers that act as advocate to their client's needs is highly desirable. We are not robots and it is worth standing out on a limb for clients. While policy reflects this, it is not necessarily fully appreciated. To not value the 'front liners' — the 'hands on' workers — is to devalue their clients too. They often need us to be their voice. While this notion may sound like a cliché, by promoting greater awareness we link the term 'disability' with 'possibility' in a meaningful way.

A basic message here is that unless we come together as a team (as policy dictates we do), then we fragment the disability system and deny the disabled the right to be heard. The voices of the lovely people presented within these pages will show you why that is so important.

ONE

"We must empower every individual with a disability to live with dignity in an inclusive society"
— William E. Lightburn

The year was 1982. I was living in Canberra and had begun the first day of placement for my welfare officer course. An enthusiastic student, I was motivated by my previous two years as a carer. During that time, I nursed my mother through a terminal illness and completed a year of voluntary work with a local health centre's program that involved visiting homebound people. From these experiences, I realised how many gaps there were in the home health care system and how many individuals were in desperate need of support. In order to understand the welfare system better, I decided it was time for some formal training.

I was not fooled by the beautiful façades of attractive houses along the neatly groomed streetscapes. I became concerned about those isolated behind closed doors, who felt unable to escape their maze of loneliness and despair, such as the young mum who was left to deal with the impact of domestic violence, including chronic back pain, a toddler, no home and no support. I was to help her with shopping. No one is immune to the hurts and disappointments of life, and anyone can become disabled by it.

Yet prejudice lingers in society about those perceived as 'not okay', and those who appear a bit different to us or those who may have fallen into a welfare web through no fault of their own often become handy targets. I know of one story where a person was denied voluntary work with the disabled, despite the organisation desperately needing more volunteers. The fear was that the volunteer may come across as condescending as he said his role would be based on his 'Christian duty'. While he meant well, the organisation thought his attitude may be reflected towards his clients, potentially causing them to feel subservient.

I felt dismayed that the organisation had dismissed him so easily. Perhaps he would have been a wonderful and valued team member, and the ten-week volunteer course may have addressed any potentially questionable motivations. I understand that each client's sense of dignity was seen as an important aspect of being able to move forward, but the 'would be' volunteer's self-esteem was ignored.

That was my first lesson in how welfare workers might be perceived as assuming a role of superiority over clients. I came across many examples of this in subsequent years between staff, carers, volunteers and the client — but that is a whole other story.

Getting back to that first day of placement. It was a cold crisp morning of minus five degrees, which promised to become clear and sunny — just a typical Canberra winter's day. I really had no idea what to expect but knew I would be busy. As I put on my trusty coat, hat and gloves, I tried not to think of small neglected children lying in wet beds in cold isolated rooms, or of pets left outside during the night.

"The key to our winters, love," a local once said, "is to find yourself somewhere behind glass by late morning and you will feel like toast."

Now that was a luxury I felt like trying as I drove away in a car that felt like an icebox, ready to embark on my first day where I would 'shadow' those in management positions at a large community centre.

I was required to write reports on everything I observed, so the main order of the day was to pay attention. I dutifully arrived at the carpark to meet my supervisor at 8.30am sharp — no time for pleasantries. I was soon confronted by Lisa, the fast-talking social worker I'd been assigned to for the day. In time, I came to recognise the dark circles around her eyes were indicative of a Department of Health worker — they generally deal with large caseloads (around forty-five each). It was apparent that the social workers were time limited in regards to each case, and often in desperate need of relief from burnout. This was more than thirty-five years ago, and I wonder if anything has changed — I doubt it.

The Canberra roads were relatively quiet for peak hour, and there was some urgency about getting to the destination prior to 9am as Lisa kept saying she hoped the large gates were open. Not wishing to buy into her frenetic energy, I decided to focus on my notes. After what seemed like ten minutes, I was brought back to attention when we stopped with a *clunk*.

"Open up, you mongrels!" Lisa yelled, trying to nudge the iron gates open with the van's bulbar.

The gates held their position defiantly. A quick assessment

told me rain was imminent and we seemed stuck there. Since no one was in sight, I decided to brave the tempestuous weather and open the gates. As soon as the car was partly through, Lisa hurriedly handed me my folder and bag and instructed me to wait over by the building, while she went to the restricted area for a short while.

In a flash she was down the road, leaving me standing alone to scan my surroundings. Above me loomed ominous grey clouds; below me silver frosted ground; and in front a towering sombre-looking Greystone complex menaced by a prickly forest of thorns. It seemed as if I'd landed in some Dickensian novel. A sudden gust of wind hit me so I took shelter near the corner of the building, under a set of tall double doors. I started to remove a sheet from my folder when a gust of wind mischievously rearranged my loose papers, tossing them around my feet. The wind then pushed me against the tall double doors. I stumbled like some comedy clown act, but thankfully managed to keep upright.

That was the moment that changed my career path. Ever since that day, I have mused at how I literally stumbled into the experience, as with that one push, the door gave way and I fell backwards into a shadowy room of many dark forms. Once my eyes adjusted and I regained my balance, I noticed the many faces turned in unison towards me. Strange 'whisperings' of gasps came from all directions.

"Oh, hello. Sorry to disturb. I think the wind wanted me to come in," I giggled apologetically.

Relieved to hear chuckling, I stood there, taking in the scene. There were about twenty-five adults sitting on rows of benches in the centre of the hall. They were arranged in two groups with half facing the other and just enough space between to allow for leg room. The group were wearing dark oversized coats — further adding to the depressing atmosphere. To my left was a half-sized person squeezed between the others, sitting with their head low, gently rocking. The people to my right shuffled along the bench, making space for me. How could I not oblige and share their wooden seating? It was a squeeze but I managed to fit.

"Well, thank you, but I'll just stay for a few minutes as my supervisor will be back soon," I said, while wondering how Lisa was going to find me.

I glanced across at the half-sized person again, hoping it wasn't a child, but I was unable to determine the age. I had no idea who these people were, but once they began asking me questions I determined they were disabled by their speech patterns.

Someone seated directly across from me asked the first question, with a barely audible voice: "Wa yu narm?"

"I'm Barbara and..." before I could draw breath, a stream of questions flew at me. Such things as "Arrr u marrd?", "Chillen?", "U dive car?", "Where u live?" came from different people. I had to tune in carefully as letters seemed to be missing from their pronunciations.

"Yes. Two. Yes." They fell quiet for a moment as I described my house. I even managed to convey that my young son was older and taller than my daughter, and that her hair was long and often plaited with different coloured ribbons such as blue, yellow, green and red to match her clothes. I shared all those small details, seeing how they appeared so focussed on my words and assuming they were starved of such trivia.

"Oh loo pitty," said one sweet voice with the sound of delight.

If I had time and the room had been better lit, I could have offered to show them photos I had in my wallet. Their interest was intense and it seemed as though I was offering them a sense of wonderment. Their imagination needed feeding, and for those few minutes, I could feel the longing for what could be. The mention of my dog caused much delight and a "woof woof" sound from the back was followed by much chuckling. For a short while we were all 'in the moment' and I realised just how much I took for granted each day — all those small and precious details of my life. But all too soon the spell was broken as an intrusive "beep beep" forced me back to my demanding world.

"Oops, that's my cue. I had better show her where I am. Thanks for the seat and chat, and lovely meeting you all. Goodbye," I blurted, already halfway out the door.

It seemed that within seconds I was back in the car, with Lisa whisking me off to our full day of planned duties. How I regretted that I had scrambled away so swiftly. Having seen how the room had lit up with a warming glow when I'd spoken of my 'ordinary' life, I knew I had impacted their lives, but sadly, I imagined them all just sitting there again in their cold dark silence. I looked back as we drove away from that bleak scene, wondering what that place was and who those people were.

"Oh, that's just part of the institution," said my supervisor, somewhat dismissively.

"Well, there were lots of people seated on rows of benches. Why would they have been sitting there so early in a freezing place, all alone in a semi-dark hall?" I asked, concerned that there may have been a shortage of power or funds for adequate heating or lighting on such a cold morning. I waited for her to tell me what this institution was.

"They're from the dorm further down the road and are waiting for their bus to take them to their job," Lisa replied with a tone that said she was keen to deal with other matters. "Most live there and have for years," was all she said.

"Do only adults live there?" I persisted, hoping she had something reassuring to say, as I couldn't bear to think a child was amongst them.

"Yes, most are, but sometimes younger ones can get placed there temporarily if there's no room elsewhere, and especially if they are in transition to be placed somewhere else, like from interstate," she added impatiently, apparently keen for me to drop my enquiry of potentially confidential information.

We seemed to be constantly moving on to the next business of the day and, despite appearances, I could tell Lisa was a good-hearted person as she let down her guard while explaining that our next stop would be a remand centre for young offenders. They could even include children as young as twelve who had been removed from dysfunctional or abusive homes. As she discussed the details of the small prison-like cell rooms the children were placed in, I noted the sadness in her voice. I discovered I had misjudged her, as her somewhat abrupt manners may have been her way of coping with her casework overload. With barely enough time to dwell on what that meant, we had to consider the next five issues that were on the agenda for the day.

"A disabled couple are expecting a baby next month and they have no home, so we need to help them find one. We are concerned at how they are going to manage as they have no family to support them at all," Lisa continued, in that same unattached tone that puzzled me. I was pleased that our society provided some support at least.

This apparently was nothing out of the ordinary and along with such issues as poverty, drug abuse, homelessness, domestic violence and isolation, there was no easy way to repair the despair lurking within what appeared to be an affluent community. I felt sad and emotionally exhausted by the information overload that welfare workers faced every day. Thankfully, I managed a short lunch break in the car while Lisa was meeting a housing official in the run-down outskirts of Canberra.

My notes were scattered about in total disarray — matching my thoughts. Sorting them would take time and determination. Headings such as 'Professionalism', 'Practicality' and 'Decision Processes' were waiting for my attention. I wondered how one can make sound judgements by rushing to the next 'case' with little or no time to pause and consider the emotional status of clients. I felt that notion difficult to digest so I scanned through the pages in search of inspiration. I did that many times during my three placements to find some guiding light, for I saw how complex and overloaded the welfare system was.

There seemed to be so many people of all ages seeking help for emotional, psychological, physical and financial assistance and not enough staff available to meet each request. I saw two sheets of paper that outlined the 'Duty Statement' for a social worker and welfare officer. It listed nineteen tasks of responsibility for the social worker and a twentieth task for the welfare officer: being 'accountable to the social worker'. I realised then that my welfare duties load would be considerable even as a student.

As I had no formal qualifications at that time, I felt I was somehow intruding in the social workers' domain, but I had little choice.

When I went to the remand centre Lisa mentioned, I had to attend a requested meeting because no one else had time. My brief was to interview a seventeen year old who had allegedly committed murder. He was taken from his small cell area and I met him in a nearby lounge. He stood before me, neatly dressed and softly spoken. He did not fit the image of an alleged murderer — such was my prejudice.

After a chat to establish how he was doing, he seemed to only want one thing: to phone his mother. Yet he was not allowed to do this. I told him I was sorry but it wasn't my decision to make. I felt horrible denying his simple request, and left that interview feeling highly conflicted, because I couldn't get my head past this teen who just wanted to talk to his mum.

While that remains one of my more 'regretful' cases as a student, my best one was something I was able to make a decision about. I had to interview a young single mum who had experienced domestic violence. She had two small children and was temporarily living in a poor-quality hotel room. She was highly anxious to have her request for a two-bed housing commission rental proposition granted. The waiting list, apparently, was huge for such dwellings. I had a criteria list to tick to determine her eligibility.

As it turned out, she did not meet one of the criteria, but she'd waited so long and there was no way I could leave that day without telling her she would get her home. Yes, tick. That was it. I did not know any of the other people on the list, but I did see her desperate young face and her children's, all looking unwell. She told me the youngest child had bad asthma and the hotel room they lived in was damp. I suspected I was not going to make a very good welfare worker after all.

"As a professional, you need to be able to 'detach' or else your emotions will suffer," my notes read.

This 'helping and caring' occupation was obviously not as simple as merely 'reaching out'. Certainly, it was important to understand the difference between 'sympathy' and 'empathy' for those in need, and when one knows the difference, support can be more appropriately offered. Unfortunately, the 'demand and supply' issue within welfare was too heavily weighted towards those in need. And, of course, from a professional standpoint, 'bending the rules' was definitely frowned upon. Clearly, I had much to learn!

TWO

"Kindness is a language that the deaf can hear and the blind can see"
— Mark Twain

In due course, I realised how the disability sector was not dissimilar to that of the social welfare system, as both groups of workers can be overworked, underrated and underpaid when they ought to be highly valued. But my first lesson was to learn how to not become too involved in the emotional tugs of those seeking support, and to manage each situation 'efficiently and professionally'. I realised that while this advice offered a wise approach to prevent a potential burnout, it was not always appropriate for me as each situation is unique. However, I found out that simple kindness was one of the most potent and crucial healing mechanisms there is, and no training or policy standards can fully convey this.

Pitying the one on the receiving end of support can promote a condescending approach, rendering the recipient feeling subservient. When I began my studies, I heard about a regrettable cliché of the 'middle-class female social worker' behaving as a 'know-all do-gooder'. When I mentioned this to my lecturer she responded with a simple message: "Well, you don't have to be one of those." *Hmm*, I thought. *Indeed not*.

As long as I did not lose sight of my own sense of dignity and worth, I felt that I could respect everyone's right to that too. Thankfully, my sense of compassion has kept me in line, rendering me more effective in support. I felt that one's duty of care should include observing the emotional makeup of each client and taking that into account as a necessary requirement for any form of assistance. Often in their time of need, the client doesn't want to be pulled along behind a guiding light, but rather be shown how to work the torch.

I will never forget a line from a poem I have since forgotten the name of. As a welfare student, I heard it recited many times on the radio, during the Year of the Disabled: "Don't cry for me, do something." Simply stated, disabled people don't need our tears. They need to be treated with respect and given reasonable opportunities equal to any individual within society.

Looking back, that first day was a whirlwind of note-taking and visiting different locations. I witnessed first-hand the staggering responsibility and pressures Department of Health workers must manage in dealing with a vast array of citizens facing a huge variety of distressing situations. Reading about troubled families with young children upset me the most — and there was much to read about. Yet my mind kept drifting back to my encounter in the institution building earlier that morning. Each time I remembered those people huddled in the cold, I reminded myself that I needed to investigate further, adding another item to my rapidly growing 'to do' list. I was on a mission, but little did I know that during our last stop, I would uncover a few potential clues.

The final meeting scheduled for the day was at a place known as an industry workshop establishment, and just like our morning visit to the institution, I had no idea such places existed. We drove into the carpark to what looked like a mess of large, ramshackle buildings that resembled an old factory complex. Once again I was left to wait in a designated area. "Some of my 'cases' are here," said Lisa, "and I need to check on them — but just wait here by this side door and someone will come and show you around."

After a few minutes, a gruff voice summoned me to enter a narrow passageway leading into a storage area. The voice belonged to a tall thin man with greying hair and a beard, wearing grey overalls and black boots. As I followed him, he introduced himself as the workshop manager. He spoke as if he was keen to be somewhere else. I was just managing to keep up with his pace through a dark passageway, and as we entered a large room with workers seated at four rows of long narrow tables, I asked him what this place was.

"Like a beehive, hey love?" said the manager, who finally introduced himself in a barely audible fashion. "Everyone here calls me Terry — no big boss status here."

I stood watching the workers for a moment, but that felt awkward and invasive, so I smiled at a few faces looking at me — although most were busily handling materials or clothing of some sort.

"We employ intellectually disabled adults to sort out second-hand clothes from charity bins that come in from all over Canberra and parts of New South Wales just over the border. We pay them a small wage, which seems to give them a lot of pride. A few behavioural issues from time to time, but they are a good lot. We are like family here really — but don't quote me on that."

Interestingly, as he spoke I saw a few faces looking at me that seemed familiar. One was a middle-aged lady who was beaming a semi-toothless smile. She was wearing the same type of oversized coat I had seen earlier that morning when the wind had blown me into that building. I could clearly see her face now, but I couldn't be sure she was one of the people who'd been huddled on those benches. She gave me a little wave with her gloved hand. It was then that I was reminded about how cold it was in the workshop. I was about to ask about the obvious lack of heating, but Terry seemed to sense my thoughts and quickly redirected me by telling me about that lady.

"That's Grace and she always feels the cold. I have to drag her coat off her in the summer. I reckon it's like her security blanket — but she's a good girl and does a good job. Come on, lovey, follow me as it's nearly home time, and I want to lock up on time today," said Terry, rushing me along.

I glanced back momentarily. *Seems like dull boring work*, I thought. *But I mustn't judge too quickly how others feel.* I didn't realise then how important that insight about making assumptions would be — especially about how important certain activities are to others. Prejudice comes in many guises.

I caught up with Terry in his office, or rather a depository for piles of paper, where a chair was hiding — somewhere. The walls were adorned with dusty posters showing schedules with old dates — some from several years earlier. There were also lists that related to incoming bags of clothes and several photos depicting past workers. In his gruff voice, Terry told me all their names like a proud grandfather. *A softy, after all*, I decided.

"Happy to stand, thanks," I said to his offer to sit on that alleged seat.

Terry became engrossed in looking for a special 'bloody blue folder'.

Most likely on that hidden chair, I mused. I'm sure he meant well, but he was probably overloaded like Lisa.

"I thought I would give you a copy of our work schedule and a bit of history of the place," Terry said. "Anyway, we have about fifty workers at any one time and there is a canteen in the adjoining building. But everyone here usually brings their own lunch. About fifty/fifty men and women, but that can vary each year. Some have been coming here for over twenty years or more," he said, still shuffling papers from one spot to another and mumbling his words.

Suddenly, Terry was silent and stood looking through the dirty window, as if he remembered something important. Then, thoughtfully and slowly, he offered a more personal view of this place and these people.

"It's like a social outlet here, love, and for many their only friendship base. You see, some live with aging parents, and others in institutions round these parts. I think it's good for 'em to feel like they are important and appreciated. Thankfully, they all mostly get on with each other, but I have a chat if I see someone who seems to be upset. Things get sorted out like that." He paused; I waited.

"Their task is to remove buttons and belts from non-reusable items that have already been sorted out further up. Others along the line of tables separate certain types of material that are to be torn or cut up to make cleaning rags, which get sold on to other industries. You could say they work in 'the rag trade' as this is a huge rag sorting workshop — it's a win-win situation, really, as many industries need rags and this place provides an opportunity for disabled people to work," he stated proud, if somewhat defensively. I wondered if this workshop notion was a contentious issue?

I heard a siren screech in the distance, followed by the sound of people shuffling about. Lisa mysteriously appeared and we said goodbye to Terry. Outside, we passed several buses as we drove back to where we began that morning. Shortly after, I drove home with far more questions than I had answers for. But written in my scramble of notes was a new 'label': Intellectual Disability. I needed to find out much more about it. I wondered how these intellectually disabled workshop workers fitted into the equation of disability. Research for another day.

The previous month before my placement, our class had to practise being disabled by choosing whether to be blind, deaf or wheelchair-bound. For a few minutes, I tried them all. The blind part generated some laughter, as I knocked into others. The deaf experience brought a degree of frustration as the simulation machine sounded so 'scratchy'. It was such a relief to turn it off completely, having been told that many deaf people hear that all the time. I couldn't bear it for just that short time. We were told that being deaf does not necessarily mean total silence, just as being blind does not always mean total blackness. Some light may be registered but not form.

Officially, I chose to be in a wheelchair and later reported on my travels along a public footpath. In particular, I took note of how many people stared at me. I did not expect to feel somewhat resentful at being looked at. It felt personal and I became strangely defensive for those who endure this all the time. My reaction was indeed food for thought. Just that one hour taught me something about feeling discriminated against and judged. But I digress again, so back to the workshop issue.

Years later in Melbourne, I read about the debates by many well-intentioned individuals on the 'gross exploitation of the disabled' who are forced into menial tasks, earning a pittance and never being able to advance their skills. These workshops (better known as sheltered workshops) were dotted about the suburbs and sometimes attached to training centres for the disabled. The debate centred on this type of work being designed as cheap labour for profit-making big businesses. The work mainly offered simple assembly and packaging tasks for items such as hardware (screws and bolts), hygiene items prior to being sterilised and various small items that required counting, sorting and packaging.

One place I worked at had a workshop in one part of the building and, more often than not, the disabled workers who engaged in other activities had also volunteered to be rostered to the workshop for one morning or afternoon per week — something they took great pride in. I also witnessed how they stood keenly with hands ready for their fortnightly pay of two dollars. Clearly that amount was just a token, as the main focus for them, so I was informed, was learning a variety of skills and getting to work as a team. This was seen as just one of the programs for training the disabled and allowing them to experience different 'life skills' opportunities. For a few, the workshop activities came under the banner of 'vocational skills' and was not considered a form of exploitation.

When asked how they would spend their pay, one said, "Buy chocolate", another said, "Magazine" and yet another loved to go shopping each week to buy wool and so on. I knew that the various skills within this range of work was rather demanding for someone who had to concentrate on counting, packing or stacking boxes. From their interactions in the workshop, the workers did not seem to consider their tasks demeaning, but rather they behaved as if they felt clever and proud — along with the added value of being paid.

"I'm a good worker," was something one man often said, who loved it when it was his turn to work a shift. I could tell he felt important and he was not alone in that.

Mind you, as with any population set, some didn't want to work so only those who chose to participate did so. But overall, a smiling sense of pride was evident in their body language as the busy workers successfully completed tasks. As one parent told me, "The sense of personal satisfaction at working like that is far better than languishing in front of a TV or being bored."

Yet I still felt a sense of confusion about the low pay, even though I was told that the monetary value was not an issue and the work was more about each person experiencing the joy of feeling useful. I never really did come to terms with the conflicting elements so I tried to concentrate on the client's point of view.

The added bonus of them earning some money was getting to go out during a 'shopping program' so they could pay 'independently' for something they wanted. New key concepts relating to 'client participation' were being formulated in those days, which set the groundwork for policy development in later years. Independent Program Plans, better known as IPPs, were the order of the day and mandatory for each client. This entailed that all relevant parties associated with a given client (parents, carer, program leader and supervisor) presided at an annual IPP meeting, where a client's preferences for participation in activities, or their potential for trying new experiences, was discussed.

This led to a formal written IPP document with the heading 'Objective-Activity-Timeline', under which was outlined the specific strategy for achieving the desired goal. This format provided a 'measurable criteria' for assessing the outcome of such activities to ensure the client's wishes, needs and potential were in focus. One example of an IPP might be that 'X will pay for his ticket at the station independently'. Or 'X will make a simple sandwich independently'. An expected date of achievement would be noted, as well as review dates set. A designated 'team leader' (now called a 'key worker') was made responsible to ensure the program was implemented according to strict protocol set by policy standards.

However, the documentation for all outcomes was a contentious issue as it was generally cumbersome and time-consuming. Unfortunately, all the extra paperwork significantly reduced quality contact between staff and client. I saw one report that gave step-by-step instructions for teaching someone to clean their teeth. It offered a 'backward chain' (starting with the end result) of 120 steps, and each one had to be ticked off in a complicated chart. The writing and reading of the endless charts took too much time up.

Was this going to work? No and no. So eventually something new was trialled in an attempt to find a streamlined form of documentation/reports. I never felt that any form of assessment document was perfect, but it did help staff focus on clients' needs and personal preferences. And in the final analysis, that was what it was all about.

Once the government began financially supporting the hugely expensive staff needed to operate the growing training centres and day programs around the state, they had to ensure their dollars were demonstrating positive focus and outcomes for all the disabled clients on their books. That is understandable and it has meant that all employed in the disability field were — and still are — made fully accountable for their roles.

Finally, staff were no longer seen as mere 'babysitters', but teachers and supervisors; courses, such as a three-year degree in disability, were established. Staff roles were now being seen as 'professional' and the expectations of those roles increased, along with staff receiving the new title Department of Disability Services Officer (DDSO). When a client engaged in a social event, for example, it was deemed necessary to justify that activity and demonstrate how a client might benefit from it. It may have been as simple as helping someone learn how to purchase a drink at a café or a more complex experience such as learning how to safely manage public transport independently.

Such tasks, while seeming basic, can be daunting and confusing to many intellectually disabled individuals. Even participation within the community was seen as an anxiety-inducing event for some, but gradually clients' confidence increased by virtue of opportunity and exposure.

Overall, the fundamental principles of those early years of change placed emphasis on client potential. People could argue back then that the establishment of sheltered workshops, for example, encouraged formal programs such as 'Money Skills'. Many clients who had no idea about the concept of money were given the opportunity to extend their knowledge and understanding by purchasing something from their own earned funds. So today, regardless of a client's presenting ability at any given time, the overriding decree is that there is always room for improvement.

It was apparent that the philosophical arguments around sheltered workshops was never fully resolved as technologies changed over time and, thankfully, by the late 1980s new rules for the disabled were decreed. Such were those early years when we saw the pendulum swing wildly in both directions with new ideas. The dynamics of change continue to this day, where there is some call for privatising the services to the disabled in Victoria. In Sydney, the process of a complete handover of some organisations to private operators has already begun. How this will translate to the benefit or detriment of the disabled is yet to be determined.

'Self-Advocacy' was yet another formal program started during the trial-and-error days. This was designed to help raise clients' awareness about their rights. It was a worthy notion that made some clients feel empowered. However, I know of one smart client who decided he had the right to choose whether he took his lunch time medication or not. He chose not to, and in doing so, there was a dramatic escalation of his challenging behaviour.

Needless to say, the administration of one's medication was hastily taken off the 'right to self-determination' list! This reminded me of when a large mental institution in a northern suburb of Melbourne was closed down and the 'patients' were given 'the right' to take their medication independently. The results were disastrous for some. Many ended up in the streets, unable to cope with the freedom of living without support.

Another program termed 'Vocational Skills' was introduced to all day program centres, with its purpose being to get everyone a job in the community. That eventually saw a rapid change of heart too — once the penny dropped after 'trialling' the idea (I relate to this situation later). I do not denigrate those brave new policymakers because in those days, everyone working in the disability field was on a huge learning curve and I am certain they were sincere with their intentions. So many ideas have come and gone, and rapid changes meant mistakes were made.

One issue is that funds for staffing annually constitutes a huge financial burden, so due to the complexity of need and individuality, it is difficult to get the systems of care just right. Unfortunately, it has often become a case of 'them' and 'us' — the policymakers versus the disgruntled staff. The ideal situation is to keep all participants in the disability field on the same page, so the clients are not being compromised with their daily care and the staff are not feeling devalued. But because there is so much to consider on many levels, it is difficult to get the balance right, even after all these years of change. Nevertheless, the saying "there is always room for improvement" is one worth repeating.

THREE

"Never ignore somebody with a disability.
You don't realise how much they can inspire you"
— Unknown

The welfare course I did helped open my eyes to many welfare matters, but I concluded that my real learning experience about disability began during my final course placement. I attended a meeting with my supervisor about the opening of a new style of residence for the intellectually disabled. This new complex of modern dwellings was set in a typical leafy Canberra surrounding, adjoining several residential suburbs. Little did I know that they were looking for staff, nor did I expect them to declare me a likely candidate. I had only offered myself to do a few voluntary hours on the weekend for the experience, but by the time the meeting was over, I had signed up for some casual work. I reasoned that it was part of my overall education and with the help of my ever-supportive husband, I could manage a few more hours a week away from home.

I was called for my first shift a few days later and over the months, I worked in all areas of the complex. Unlike the dormitory accommodation of the old style large institutions, these modern dwellings had bedrooms for each resident, enabling personal items to adorn their private rooms. With a large shared dining room, the dwellings were set up to look like inviting and comfortable homes, with two indoor living areas and a covered patio. Each section catered for a different age and gender group. I mainly worked in the section with adult males and it was there, on my first day, that I thought I saw someone familiar to me.

It took me a few days to find out all the residents' stories, and I found out the youngest, Robbie, had been transferred from Sydney after his elderly aunt had died. I was told that he had been placed temporarily in an old institution in Canberra to wait for the opening of a purpose-built residential complex of separate housing units. I wondered if this young man was the half-sized person I had seen in the dark building on my first day of placement. Confidentiality policies prevented me from knowing his previous address so I was never sure. At least I had the opportunity to get to know this young man better. A man of few words, he appeared to understand what I said and seemed to appreciate my attention. In particular I learned he liked music, as when ABBA played on the radio, he would stand close to the music, smiling and sometimes quietly repeating, "Like ABBA."

As this activity seemed to provide him with much joy, the staff decided to use some of Robbie's disability pension to purchase a small portable cassette tape player, plus a range of tapes, including ABBA, Elvis Presley and the Bee Gees — with the permission of the administrator in charge of his funds, of course. However, he only wanted to play the ABBA tape over and over. We found it gave him great comfort, as he always seemed content and ready to smile when he had the small machine nearby — usually in his hands.

If he needed to turn it off for something, such as being at the dinner table, the staff would explain respectfully why he needed to turn it off and he understood. This was formally written in his profile folder to ensure that the correct protocol was observed by all staff.

A year or more later, my family and I moved back to Melbourne, our hometown. Within a few months, I decided to do extra studies in psychology and some casual work at a local facility for intellectually disabled adults. To my surprise, I found Robbie was there, having moved to Melbourne at his uncle's request. Sadly, they never met as his uncle died a few days after Robbie moved into a suburban group home, which was fully staffed and purpose-equipped for five disabled residents. This type of accommodation is a common feature in many suburbs in and around Melbourne, but there is a large waiting list for residency.

After settling in to his new abode, Robbie began a full-time day placement at the local centre where I worked. It was there, on a busy day, that I experienced a 'magic moment' with him.

That rainy winter's day had many colourful umbrellas moving against the grey sky, and it seemed as though rainbows were waving amongst us. I was supervising the usual scurry of arrivals via taxi, bus and car delivering the eighty or so 'trainees' to their day placement centre. Their ages ranged from early twenties to early fifties, with an equal mix of genders. The morning was relatively uneventful as the groups of about ten, supported by their team leaders, met in different areas for their assigned hourly classes.

The eight plus staff, formally designated as 'instructors', were required to wear several 'expert' hats each day, teaching such skills as literacy, numeracy, cooking, money handling, communication, gardening, arts and crafts, and self-advocacy. There was also an eclectic mix of social programs, including swimming and fortnightly horse-riding sessions with an organisation called Pegasus.

By midday, many of the trainees had gathered in the large dining room, where they would sit for morning tea and lunch. The only variation to this particular day was that a new staff member was asked to assist with dining duty. This task involved helping trainees with their drinks, making sure they had their lunches with them, and general supervision. I was busy upstairs, dealing with paperwork and hoping I'd get a lunch break in a few minutes. And that was when events unfolded rapidly — and very loudly!

I had already moved towards the sounds of screaming and smashing glass when I heard a frantic voice shout for me to hurry down. By the time I rushed down the two long ramps, the area of devastation, evidenced by an upturned chair or two and broken glass scattered about the floor, was deserted. The diners had clearly scurried away in fright as only silence greeted me. As I scanned the scene, I wondered what had been responsible for this unfortunate turn of events, and then I noticed a clue: a multi-coloured lunch box lying on the floor, broken in two pieces. It belonged to Robbie.

A nervous voice behind me offered, "He's gone around the side of the workshop."

It was an area that no one used much, other than to deposit some junk or store the rubbish bins. It was an uninviting space — shaded and narrow — between the shed and high wire fence. As I turned the corner I saw in that dull light, seated on a rickety wooden bench, a small man with his head lowered, rocking and staring at his empty hands.

Calmly, I asked, "Are you okay, Robbie?"

"Obbie upset," was all he uttered, still rocking himself.

We had often shared his cute version of his name with light hearted humour but not now. I sat next to him and focussed on the telling sign that his precious cassette player was missing, the meaning of which was well understood by the usual staff. It seemed highly likely that some relevant information had not been conveyed to the new staff member.

Thankfully, there was no blood visible on Robbie's hands, although a visit to the first aid room was in order. But for now, the most immediate need was to be sure this troubled young man was no longer a danger to himself or anyone else. With him still puffing out the tail-end of his rage, I offered this: "We'll get your music back soon, Robbie, after we sit here for a few minutes to help you relax. Okay?"

"Yes, sit here — get music back soon."

We sat for a while without speaking, with me providing Robbie with a reassuring presence. I had come to know Robbie's emotional motivations well and this event reminded me of how misunderstandings or lack of appropriate knowledge can lead to a sense of confusion, frustration, and potentially result in unwanted behaviours. If, for example, someone took Robbie's cassette player off him during lunch without assuring him he'd get it back, that could spell disaster, with Robbie panicking. In such situations, rage can so easily be confused with an expression of fear.

After a few seconds of silence, Robbie was deep in contemplation, mumbling quietly to himself. Knowing much of his history, I presumed how events might have unfolded during his lunch time, while he ate his sandwich and listened to his music.

I could imagine he may well have told it this way: *I often seem to be in dark places where I feel anxious and confused. When someone new is with me, I feel scared that they won't know what I need. I don't know what happened before. I had my music playing — perhaps I put the dial up too loud again. Someone took it away, and I could hear loud screaming close by, and when I realised it was coming from me I felt scared as I didn't know how to stop. I don't know how the chair broke the window either. Everyone was running away. I wanted to run too. I feel safe now, but I don't know what to do. I am glad she will help me get my music.*

With the sombreness of this space, Robbie's memories may have flooded back to another time previously in Canberra when he potentially felt unsure and alone while being seated in a darkened place (assuming he was the half-sized person I saw that day). I was also there that time so reasoned if I entered his thoughts, we could share the experience once again, but this time from his version of the events.

We all seemed to be waiting for something, all huddled together on hard benches. It was a strange place and all the others were so much bigger than me. I don't know how old I was because I don't understand about numbers. But some seemed friendly and smiled at me. I had no music then and no one spoke much so, apart from hearing a few strange noises around, I used to sit in lots of silence. I always liked to rock myself as it helps me feel calm. Then something strange happened.

It was very cold in that place. I felt scared of the loud wind as it kept rushing to get inside the broken window. It sounded angry and kept flapping and slapping the torn curtains as it came through a hole in the glass. Then someone seemed to crash through the big doors at the front and I got a fright. A lady was stumbling in but I could tell she was nice because she was giggling. I liked how she talked to us in that friendly way and all the things she told us. She never spoke to me and I wanted her to. But she hurried away. I felt sad then but I met her again at that new place, and now she works here too and I see her often. I feel safe with her — she understands about my music too.

Robbie was too engrossed in his thoughts to look up.

I don't know what's wrong with me, but I don't walk like lots of people I see, and I make strange sounds when I feel scared or when strangers stare at me. Someone asked me once if I had parents, but I don't know about that. I never said 'mum' or 'dad' to anyone. Maybe there was something wrong with me when I was a baby. I remember a lady who took care of me when I was a little boy. She used to hold my hand and gave me hugs. It felt good and I think it was what love feels like. But she left me and then lots of different people looked after me. It wasn't the same — but at least I have ABBA *now.*

I broke the silence by suggesting it was time to go, but first we had to clear up some of the mess and then get his cassette. I felt sure he needed a drink too, so we walked from the side of the building towards the dining room, and I realised someone had already cleared up the mess. We kept walking and looked through the dining room's full length window. I directed Robbie's attention to his peers, who were once again seated.

Robbie stood shoulder height to me and was swaying, smudged tears clinging to his flushed cheeks as he peered inside. I pointed out the different coloured coats everybody was wearing. I named a few, saying the colours resembled the rainbow umbrellas that so busily moved about during the morning rush. Robbie contemplated the scene for a while then quietly declared, "Rainbow people."

FOUR

"Everybody is a genius. But if you judge a fish by its ability to climb a tree, it will live its whole life believing it is stupid"
— Albert Einstein

As I journeyed through the next thirty or more years, I witnessed how my clients had so many endearing unique qualities, as well as some presenting a complex array of 'shadow-colours', which carried a psychiatric 'overlay'. Each client was categorised under the banner 'Intellectually Disabled' (ID). Later, I came to learn that, psychologically speaking, we like to put labels on anything that does not seem the norm, which is a function of the formal 'support' process.

Naturally, the practical value of assessment means that it becomes a formal 'identifying' source. So, like it or not, the label does have benefits towards a whole range of assistance, especially financially. Without this process, it can become difficult to know what measures are most appropriate for a given individual. I have seen how it benefits those in need of various forms of support. Often if a client presents as borderline, this 'identification' process can take a long time. I know of one case that took two years while the family struggled financially and emotionally.

These labels cover different categories indicative of a vast array of a person's 'inabilities'. These may be things such as not being able to manage a job independently, handle money, manage one's anger when feeling fearful or highly anxious, or control one's behaviour in an ongoing way. Individuals need to demonstrate a range of such 'conditions' or a certain level of cognitive capacity in order to qualify for an ID pension.

Unfortunately, fear and ignorance — a legacy of our past — has meant that being intellectually disabled is fraught with misconceptions of what it means. So let's go back a step or three to see how matters evolved with the three main headings of disability — Mental, Physical and Intellectual — and how they may interrelate. From my work perspective, this has formed the basis of my experiences, as some of my clients have endured all three disabilities, with varying degrees in awareness of their differences.

Most of us know the archaic term 'lunatic', which related to a whole range of mental health issues that were often misunderstood. These days, with a greater sense of political correctness, we avoid such terms, but I still hear them now and then from those who are not mindful of how such words may impact those born with a cognitive or physical disability.

The 'softer touch' words, such as 'abnormal' or 'subnormal', were later used to describe concerning behaviours with no insight to the cause or a remedy. Incarceration was mostly how people dealt with unusual aberrant behaviours, claiming it was to 'protect' the 'afflicted' individuals and their community. This gave rise to locking away many who simply may have appeared different to 'the norm'.

Mind you, the official meaning of 'normal' cannot be pinned down by any serious psychological debate, so maybe we are too sanctimonious about our own relative normal status. I remember one year during my studies at a Melbourne University that the psychology department reserved a semester to explore this topic and concluded that due to a whole range of presenting variabilities from one end of the bell curve to the other (a statistical analysis tool used in research), we could not possibly give a definitive answer to the question, 'What is normal?'

The best we have come up with in our society is the development of the intelligence quotient (IQ) measure. For example, a score of a hundred means 'average intelligence' — although in recent years, even emotional or creative intelligence is considered as equally valid in some schools of thought.

From my sociological research years ago, I learned about a detailed, but rare, interview with an aged Aboriginal man known as James (Jimmie) Barker (1900-1972). The interview tapes were edited by Janet Mathews and published as *The Two Worlds of Jimmie Barker* in 1977. Jimmie related the repressive discipline and denigration of Aboriginal culture at the mission school he attended as a child, where a restricted 'white man's' syllabus was taught in the segregated setting.

Being pitted intellectually against an otherwise all-white class of children, he was accused of being dim-minded as he flunked the IQ test. Yet the test was designed for white society, and the teacher did not take into consideration Jimmie's cultural background. Already ostracised for his skin colour, and then for his mental capacity, what hope did he and others like him have to express their true selves in such an environment? Years later, Jimmy spoke with dignity, wisdom and great insightfulness.

Now, while this represents quite a different situation, the

principle is the same — there is merit in helping any person with an ID diagnosis to find what they are good at. If, for example, they cannot dress themselves, this does not mean they couldn't possibly have any talents. It could be some craft, gardening or a simple task such as sorting. It may be that they are brilliant at music or art. They often don't know what talents or skills they may have until they're given the opportunity to try different experiences. I have observed a whole range of remarkable skills performed by those who would otherwise have been denied expression without recognition of their abilities. We still know very little about how the brain can produce such diversity of talents, yet we are masters of negative prejudice and discrimination.

Just consider if the young Jimmy had his IQ tested for knowledge about tracking, how to survive alone in the wild, how to find food in a vast bush area, not to mention how to read the seasons to benefit and respect the earth. Any Aboriginal child may well have taught his white Mission school teachers much about such skills. However, it seems that psychologically speaking, we get to feel more superior when we can denigrate someone else. And let us not forget that irrespective of our IQ level, any one of us can potentially develop a mental or physical disability, and such experiences would not render us as 'not okay'. No one is ever immune to experiencing serious 'down times'. If we were honest, we could all claim to have experienced a degree of physical, emotional or psychological difficulty at some point in our life.

Thankfully, these days, the concept and conversation of mental illness is crawling out of the shadows, with certain celebrities publically revealing their plight. However, exhibiting aberrant behaviour generally remains a highly disrespected status, despite its wide prevalence throughout all communities across the globe — regardless of IQ level or financial status. Such confronting issues may include a diagnosis of clinical depression, bi-polar disorder, psychosis under the umbrella of schizophrenia, acute anxieties, obsessive compulsive disorder, autism spectrum disorder, anorexia, etc. Then add a range of issues under the 'learning difficulties' and dementia banner and you have a list that seems to be growing in our society.

During the 1950s, America began formally categorising disabilities of all kinds to help guide clinicians and researchers. Named the *Diagnostic and Statistical Manual of Mental Disorders* (DSM-5), this medical model of diseases is now up to its fifth edition. It was developed to provide standard criteria for the diagnosis and identification of a myriad of disabilities, and this system of classifications, while not without its critics, has a new edition that includes more conditions than ever before. In his *A Critique of the DSM*, Karl Tomm, M.D, suggests it is an "inadvertent pathologising influence in our culture". Some professionals infer that the DSM has become a labelling process that can initiate permanent stigmatising within the vast range of our social interactions.

While I am no expert on such matters, the question we may well ask is what is the alternative? So the debate about labels continues and, for now, it will be our main tool for determining levels of support given. Nevertheless, there are many individuals who are relieved to finally have some label applied to their specific affliction after years of struggling with something no one could provide a formal diagnosis for.

As difficult as revelations of their private selves are for

those afflicted individuals, their sharing is valued for the benefit of greater exposure and education. The World Health Organisation (WHO) acknowledges that the institutional style of care (based on a medical model) has led to human rights violations, dependency and a lack of opportunities for rehabilitation. Thankfully, these days, alternative modes of community support are offered. The imperative rests with greater transparency and public knowledge having a tremendous impact on how individuals and societies deal with this global crisis of mental illness's many forms.

Past experts, many of whom participated in those dreaded asylum years, were presumably well-intentioned and so initiated a move away from how they managed those denizens of despair who wasted away in harsh neglect. Nevertheless, it is not surprising that the fog of stigmatisation, discrimination, misinformation, ignorance and fear in our modern world is only recently gradually lifting.

Five

"What lies behind us and what lies before us are tiny matters compared to what lies within us"
— Ralph Waldo Emerson

This legacy of 'madness' — once associated with possession by demons — seems difficult to be extricated from our genetic sensibilities. However, it is the case that many famous people were found to have experienced a form of aberrant mental condition during some part of their life. Isaac Newton, born in 1643, who became known as the world's most influential scientist, was said to have been emotionally harmed at an early age by his parents' separation. One bibliography stated that he did not speak until he was eight, and by age nine began to show pronounced psychotic tendencies. It was suggested that the trauma of his early years carried on through his long brilliant career, with his intermittent expression of obsessive anxieties and irrational violent outbursts.

Fortunately, Newton was in a position to receive an education, so his genius was enabled to be expressed and flourish. I wonder how many geniuses may well have been (or are) undiscovered simply because of their relative poverty; how many potentially brilliant individuals are left languishing in institutions without a support base because they were not behaving 'normally'?

Another brilliant mind that was enabled to flourish was scientist Albert Einstein, who, as a child, was considered to have rather 'odd' behaviours. According to various bibliographies on Einstein, his potentially autistic tendencies were 'accommodated' by his many admirers and supporters once he was an adult. He often arrived at his lectures with one sock missing and his appearance dishevelled. Few may know he had a son who was diagnosed with schizophrenia. An SBS documentary on his life suggested that he had a daughter born severely disabled who was never seen publicly and assumed to have died at a young age. Mind you, this remains a contentious issue and I only raise it to highlight our propensity to hide anything that does not appear normal.

I wondered about this when I once dealt with a client who was severely intellectually disabled, yet had two siblings, a niece and a nephew who were 'gifted'. There are many historical examples of how closely aligned 'genius' and 'madness' can be; yet with selective discrimination of the famous, so often their 'differences' may be 'respectfully' overlooked. The saying goes that if one seems strange but is wealthy, then they are considered merely 'eccentric'. But if strange and poor, then they are plain old mad, sad or even bad — a good case for how discreetly our culture allows selective prejudice.

Obviously, a physical expression of disability is more visible, and one may experience a wide range and degree of physical deficits from common compromised eyesight or hearing, to being wheelchair bound. Nevertheless, there are many who feel reluctant to confess they need to wear glasses or a hearing aid, or even use a walking frame, for fear of 'showing their age'. Such is the innate nature of feeling discriminated against, as if we can only be judged positively if we are a perfect specimen.

So it comes as no surprise that any person who presents as different may feel as though they are perceived negatively. The way our society deals with individual differences may relate directly to feelings of our deep sense of self-worth. We want to be accepted by our peers and 'fit in'. We are driven by our perceptions of what beauty and perfection is and based on a conceptual framework that is biased and flawed. The truth is, and must we not forget, with any form of disability not one of us is immune.

Like mental illness, ID is not always visible but often it becomes obvious, due to many experiencing a dual or triple disability. Over the years, I have found that ID is highly misunderstood as many don't know how it fits into the wider scheme of disability. ID is characterised by varying degrees of limitation of cognitive functioning and adaptive behaviours for practical and social skills. This means those with ID have difficulty with some simple daily tasks involving self-care, finding direction, communication, learning new things, concentrating, understanding concepts or deficits in socialising ability, as well as potentially being more prone to a whole range of medical ailments. One can be either born with a genetic neurological deficit or disabled as a result of disease, malnourishment, neglect, environmental factors such as exposure to toxins, or by an accident.

The term 'mental retardation' was used to describe people with those disabling challenges until it changed to intellectual disability. Such genetic disorders as Down syndrome, fragile X syndrome, Williams syndrome, Prader-Willi syndrome, cerebral palsy and the autism spectrum, etc, all qualified as these may relate to crucial 'developmental delays'. They are given this label as it is not always obvious until a child has passed a developmental milestone that they can be properly assessed for an ID label. This is because the disability becomes evident during a developmental period around age eighteen months, but then can only be considered as 'developmentally delayed'. Later, the formal formula for the ID consideration is having an IQ of 70 or less for a mild ID, 50-70 for a moderate ID, and 20 or less for a severe ID. It is not always the case that a young child given a developmental delay diagnosis is necessarily later assessed as being intellectually disabled.

The relevance of this early assessment is to ensure a child is able to access intervention programs as early as possible. For babies born with a neurological problem, early interventions during the crucial developmental periods can help improve their quality of life. The level of ID varies greatly as well, and while some do also have a mental and/or physical disability, many present as having a low IQ and often seem somewhat child-like in their cognitive capacity. Mind you, that largely means their brains did not develop beyond the IQ of a child, perhaps of age three or age ten, for example. Some mildly ID adults have been able to manage simple daily tasks such as hygiene, shopping, basic food prep, washing or other domestic chores as most twelve year olds may do. There are some adults with ID who are able to live independently with back up support, while many others require twenty-four hour supervision.

In the past, for some who were diagnosed with ID, only a

basic standard of independence at best may be their long-term outcome. However, this is not to suggest that any individual cannot learn and grow throughout their lives.

With new discoveries in the science of brain plasticity, we know now that we can explore the potential of anyone at any age, given the opportunity. Ongoing learning is encouraged for those of all ages and disability. But early intervention is crucial as modern psychology has much to say about neglected conditions for brain development and resulting long-term detriment. And that is not even talking about those who suffered in institutions, receiving little or no personal attention.

Unfortunately, about a third of the three per cent of Australians who are ID-diagnosed are within the lowest range of the set IQ standard, and my concern has been the amount of attention given to early intervention. Over the earlier years, I could see the percentage of government funding towards that youngest age group (2-6) was disproportionately lower than the funding offered to adults. So often community groups have lamented the funding shortfalls to their wonderful early learning programs and are desperate to enable families on low incomes to access the programs cheaply or freely. Put simply, if those family groups could not afford to access those programs, then those babies and young children may well have missed out on that vital development window for their best opportunity, and thus potentially required even greater assistance (and greater financial cost to the community) as older individuals.

I've been terribly disappointed in successive governments over the time I have worked in the disability field, for not ensuring all children have this crucial attention when they need it. Often by the time they can formally be considered ID, or even developmentally delayed, they are already well into the system of dependent care, and in need of even greater support. It may well be that some very young children, had they been provided with full early developmental support, may not have needed the support services required once reaching adulthood. Hopefully, the message is getting through, but as I write this book, the welfare dollar seems to be even more stretched as economic management becomes more difficult for successive government to control.

However, it must be said that support funding for special schools helps many families navigate the education system of young children with developmental delays, including children on the autism spectrum, to a significant extent. Likewise, a special one-on-one teacher's aide for a child with a learning difficulty is often provided within a mainstream school. Yet this too is limited to funding availability.

The programs for disabled adults have improved these days, resulting in a better quality of living, and this is evidenced by the many positive changes I have witnessed first-hand since the closure of large mental health institutions. One positive outcome meant residents could move from large dormitory accommodation to their own room. Unfortunately, the legacy of the former left one client I knew with a lifelong fear and anxiety of someone coming into her space and taking her things. The damage had been done for that lovely soul.

Overall, Australia can stand tall about how we support the disabled in general, as many other less advanced countries are still managing their disabled in relative poverty and neglect. Only time will tell how well the newly formed

National Disability Insurance Scheme (NDIS) is received by the disabled community as we move into new territory of funding for their support, but already I hear grumblings of relative discontent. It may take a while to see potential serious shortfalls to those who were registered as in need of assistance (via the disability support pension) prior to its establishment. I suspect that when problems become evident, new policies will be modified or adjusted to ensure the disabled don't miss out on vital attention to their overall needs. Fortunately, the disabled have many who will fight for their rights.

My concern is related to the concept of an applicant being means-tested for eligibility. While funds within the family may well be available for some disabled individuals (thus excluding them from some extra support), the question is who will take responsibility for that person with regards to their development potential? Not every person or family — despite their bank balance — is able to cope or manage with their disabled family member. We will need to wait and see how NDIS is received by the wider community and how the 'voices' of the disabled, those most vulnerable in our community, are heard.

For many years, and even now with the general public, what constitutes ID was misunderstood and therefore could be as equally feared as any form of mental illness.

Once, someone asked me if I was afraid when working with 'them' and asked when my clients stopped being referred to as 'patients'. I said the change began once it was realised that someone with a disability shouldn't be thought of as having some disease. To that person, it seemed an innocent enough question, but even asking it carried a sad reflection of past attitudes. The connotations directly connect with the burden imposed on all who were interned. Even in these modern times, certain attitudes can have some disabled people feel a sense of isolation and relative neglect of their needs.

As I said previously, all too often many who presented as 'different' or displayed strange behaviour were removed from view, no matter what the cause. I once worked with a client from a very wealthy family who had placed their young disabled child, Lydia, in the hands of a large institution in another state. I first met Lydia when she was in her late fifties, but thankfully she was living within the new residential home and cared for by excellent staff, so she appeared happy enough, but I noticed how much she longed for her annual visit from her sibling who lived interstate. No matter what day or what she was doing, Lydia always mentioned that relative's impending visit — even if almost a year away.

Such was the apparent sense of shame at having a disabled offspring. In days gone by, the standard recommendation to families of disabled babies was to place them in institutions. It all represented society's prevailing attitude. And unfortunately when many of the large institutions closed down, it was too late for some of the individuals who'd been locked away for years, as they'd become too 'institutionalised' and fearful of change.

Upon closure of one large institution, approximately a third of the residents were moved to nursing homes, while the other two-thirds were divided into the smaller secluded institution, which I know still exists, or to one of the many newly formed purpose-built residences that sprang up in many quiet Australian suburban streets. Both types of accommodation offer substantial improvements to the manner in which the occupants spend their day (including attending day placement programs in the community) and generally residing in medium to high standard conditions. Who would have thought those occupants of your neighbour's home may once have been part of a great tragedy.

SIX

"It is a lonely existence to be a child with a disability that no one can see or understand; you exasperate your teachers, you disappoint your parents and worst of all you know you are not stupid"
— Susan Hampshire

If you saw the movie *One Flew Over the Cuckoo's Nest*, then you will be familiar with the way the 'inmates' functioned in those large institutions. This was not a fabrication, and, if anything, the film may have downplayed the horrors that many of the 'inmates' felt. Often, 'dubious' justification for entry to those places meant that too many individuals of all ages were lost to society. My experience of one such sad place was as a visitor during my welfare course in 1983. Along with my fellow students, I was conveyed by bus to a huge complex located in Goulburn NSW, some way out of Canberra. It was opened in 1895 and known as the Kenmore Hospital for the Insane — later known as the Kenmore Lunatic Asylum.

The numerous buildings within the vast seventy-five hectares of grounds housed the greatest numbers during the 1960s. In those years, over 1400 'inmates' were languishing there at any one time; they had been placed there for psychiatric assessment and often questionable experimental treatments. The range of psychotropic drugs available now, such as lithium and chlorpromazine, were not available back then.

The old style services eventually wound down by the early 2000s. Now, Kenmore is a site for ghost tours, but it also holds memories kept by interested and respectful people who care about its history and may have had relatives there at some point. I can well imagine their sentiments, as when I visited that day, I saw many lost souls being viewed like freaks at a side show. I wanted to know their history and why they were there. Did they have relatives? Did they get visitors? Was there someone out there who loved them or even remembered them? I was relieved to not run into any children, who would have been housed in different buildings. Yet in my mind's eye, I saw them all — blank faces with missing smiles — and I wondered what kind of a future they would have.

That day we were ushered through the long hall, past tiny glassed rooms that afforded absolutely no privacy to the 'patients' in their beds, every one of them appearing dazed.

"Oh, they have all had their zaps today," said the guide in a matter of fact way.

He was referring to electroconvulsive therapy, better known as electric shock treatment. At one point, I looked directly at a middle-aged lady's resigned face and mouthed 'sorry', feeling horrid I had looked her way.

Having no privacy, they seemed resigned or defeated. I wondered how many of them may have previously expressed their anger, fear or confusion about their plight with rage in a loud or violent manner. My cynical self can only presume they would have needed to be 'subdued', resulting in a more manageable patient. But perhaps, if I was feeling kinder towards that form of therapy, then I might have even suggested that well-intentioned staff wanted them to feel less fearsome of their surroundings.

We finally arrived at the end of the long hallway and stepped into a large room where we were greeted by one staff amongst too many patients. It seemed as though there were thirty people standing or wandering around the cold room, which was sparsely decorated with a hard wooden floor and a few old chairs and benches placed around the walls. The narrow barred windows revealed little natural light, but at the far wall stood the one potential giver of joy: a well-worn piano.

My gaze locked on a young woman in her early twenties with the natural beauty of perfect features, which in different circumstances could have ensured her model or movie star status. Yet there she stood very still in a straitjacket with her arms bound behind her. I asked the staff member why she was like that and immediately regretted it. He untied the leather straps binding her and she instantly grabbed one, pushing most of it into her mouth before he could stop her. She was quickly strapped up again, rendering her secure and silent — it seemed as if she wasn't there at all. Everything happened in a flash and I was left thinking I'd imagined it. Yet it remains a vivid sad memory to this day.

I also saw a middle-aged man with long tangled hair and no facial expression, just sitting, staring and rocking. I know from my studies that rocking is a natural mechanism to help soothe a person from the troubled waters lashing about deep within. I was told that he was brought in many years prior as a child, along with three other siblings, after being found fending for themselves around a small isolated bush shack, where their parents lay deceased.

Apparently, it was not unusual to find children abandoned or neglected deep within the bush. So without any other means of support, those children had nowhere else to go other than to live in that institution. What potential may they have demonstrated given a different chance to learn skills? That man's siblings had passed away and there he sat without ever saying a word. Had he been able to communicate, what stories might he have told? We can only wonder.

We were informed that the institution offered various recreational activities — such as music, gardening and art — which served as 'therapies' to help soothe the troubled minds of those 'inmates' and prevent boredom and loneliness. I can well imagine there were wonderfully artistic individuals amongst them — people who once had dreams — whose talents were lost to the world for the rest of their lives.

During our escorted travels, I noticed some beautiful coloured baskets for sale that the patients had made. Many were discarded to one side — *much like those who had weaved them*, I thought. I bought one with a bottle holder on the side. Now that was inventive thinking. I often wondered who had made it — a potential genius perhaps — and what they were thinking while they wove in that extra holder, such an unusual feature for any basket. I have never seen one like it since.

I feel hopeful there were caring staff working there over the years, and maybe some patients even found a degree of peace from anxieties or personal troubles. But historic records tell there was also brutality there. Kenmore, like so many other institutions, was self-contained and situated away from towns, which I believe prevented outsiders from hearing the prisoners' screams.

I did some research later about Kenmore and why someone may have been admitted to such a place. It was heartbreaking to consider how easy it was then to be perceived as a misfit in society. For example, while some would have presented with acute psychiatric symptoms, and clearly in need of support, for many the causes were unknown and treatments were often aimed at subduing or controlling any aberrant behaviours.

To be seen as suitably dysfunctional and in line for electric shock treatment, one may have been suffering from such experiences as homosexuality or postnatal depression — with added acute anxieties after having been wrenched from their newborn. Being troublesome with inebriation was also considered worthy of admission, as was having a learning disorder. So presenting drunk or disorderly, or being unable to cope at school, may well have resulted in a person being incarcerated. While so many conditions were not fully understood, it was considered problematic to society. Perhaps many concerned loved ones simply needed help to cope with their troubled family members, and hoped 'medical experts' could restore them to health. But formal admission was infinitely easier than leaving.

Considering how dire matters were in those large institutions, with the eclectic mix of afflictions, it is not surprising to see the meaning of 'disability' blurred to a large degree. Although one might be able to differentiate between the mental, physical and intellectual aspects of any disability, there may have been confusion as to what was wrong. Over the years, it has been common to meet those with ID that resulted as part of a genetic factor, which also rendered them with a physical disability, and who later developed a mental illness.

It does not take much imagination to understand how conditions of neglect, isolation, or even abuse could so easily tip the balance for someone who already has an ID to cross the line into experiencing a psychiatric ailment. However, the issues remain too complex to fully understand.

But it gets trickier too, as sometimes a person who cannot walk or talk could still be highly intelligent; for example, a person with cerebral palsy who has no control over their motor skills or an autistic person who has never spoken may well be misunderstood. Even if someone is not able to do anything for themselves due to some spasticity, it does not mean they don't have awareness of their condition and needs; they can still feel emotions deeply, have opinions or formulate complex thoughts they want to communicate with words. Appearances lead us to presume too much, which leads to false assumptions. As a consequence, we can easily miss wonderful opportunities to help someone explore their full potential. I have come across this many times with my own work.

There was a recent article in *The Age* on 20 May 2016 entitled 'This nonspeaking teenager wrote an incredibly profound letter explaining autism', which was about a fourteen year old boy who had been non-speaking all his life. Here is a tiny part of the boy's letter: "This letter is not a cry for pity... I love myself just the way I am, drunken toddler body and all. This letter is, however, a cry for attention, recognition and acceptance."

The article went on to say that his parents had no idea their son had such strong opinions about the treatment of autistic people. Apparently, he learned to use a 'rapid prompting method', a relatively new communication technique developed for people with severe autism. According to the article, he has gone on to using an advanced method called a QWERTY keyboard. But the earlier method uses assisted pointing to letters on an alphabet board; this was presented many years ago by Dr Rosemary Crossley (A.M., M.Ed., Ph.D.). During the 1980s, this method — formally known as Facilitated Communication (FC) — became highly controversial.

Dr Crossley used FC to help a little girl named Anne McDonald who was in desperate need for someone to know how smart she was. Anne was Dr Crossley's inspiration for her book *Annie's Coming Out*, which was later made into a film. During the 1980s, Dr Crossley once attended a facility I worked at so I met her personally. As dedicated and sincere as she was, she eventually had to battle for her method to gain credibility. In later years, when she had to defend FC in order to verify that Anne did indeed communicate, it was Anne herself who proved the method's validity beyond dispute in the Supreme Court of Victoria. What a profound revelation that was.

For a time, Anne managed to 'write' independently by pointing with the help of an arm support, but it proved too painful and exhausting for her; she reverted to her old method of having someone else support her arm as she pointed to the alphabet, which was the contentious issue. But ultimately, research suggests FC rests on sound scientific footing. Ramp Up — an ABC disability, discussion, debate group — cite two of the largest studies (Cardinal et al, 1996, and Bernadi and Tuzzi, 2011) that offer support for FC and provide clear evidence validating this claim.

When dealing with the disabled, who are all too often in vulnerable positions, anything can be subject to abuse, including FC. However, that does not in any way denigrate or negate a wonderful system that provides hope for those intelligent beings who are unable to communicate. Dr Crossley's achievements deserve admiration for what she achieved for the disabled, all of which can be researched in places like DEAL (Dignity, Education, Advocacy and Language), a communication centre in Melbourne that was renamed the Anne McDonald Centre. While Dr Crossley promoted and worked tirelessly as the director of this organisation, it is the story of little Anne — the toddler she rescued and later adopted — that provides for a most poignant, yet graphic, message to us all. Here is just a little of her story.

Anne McDonald, one of five siblings, was born in 1961 with severe cerebral palsy. She could not walk, talk or feed herself and was sent to the Victorian Commission Institution for Disabled Children Hospital in Melbourne at age three. In her autobiography, she wrote about her early years at the institution, which she described as a "state garbage bin". Tragically, very young children were taken in to care there regardless of their level of intelligence. She claimed that they were disfigured, distorted and often disturbed due to the neglected state they were left in.

Anne wrote about how babies would lie on the floor or in a cot all day without therapy, education, personal possessions or toys, and were given absolutely no attention. Anne only weighed twelve kilograms at age sixteen due to neglect and starvation. Rosemary Crossley gave her a chance for a new life and Anne later described herself as "the lucky one".

That hospital, along with other institutions, eventually

closed with the patients being distributed throughout other community facilities. Concerned staff such as Rosemary, who once worked there as a nurse, could relate to the irony of it being located just ten minutes from Parliament House in Melbourne. While the health professionals of the day, who promoted the biomedical models of categorising distress, made strides on mental health in general, these helpless disabled babies were not even considered for social/environmental avenues of therapy. It was unthinkable how those children were denied even a tiny measure of pleasure. All not that long ago.

As time went on, Anne's life unfolded with many achievements and she became well-known around the world. She passed her HSC, earned a degree in humanities from Deakin University in 1994, and enjoyed an active social life with her friends. She travelled overseas and was a guest speaker at many venues and awarded the personal achievement award in the 2008 National Disability Awards, after being an advocate for the rights of people without speech. Despite her success and accolades, Anne considered herself "just a normal person with normal courage".

Anne died in 2010, after thirty plus years of care and loving devotion from Rosemary and her partner. Anne's legacy is encapsulated in the words on her plaque at the Melbourne General Cemetery: "If other people without speech are helped as I was helped, they will say more than I could say. Free the imprisoned."

SEVEN

"I alone cannot change the world, but I can cast a stone across the waters to create many ripples"
— Mother Theresa

During the late 1980s, I was working in a facility that offered day programs for ID adults. Many of the people who attended had known each other for years, even from early childhood. The problem for many parents with disabled children during those days of the large institutions was that they had no alternative other than to care for them. They were faced with this extra pressure, over and above the many difficulties and complexities of needing to care for their other children and the general day to day domestic load.

The wonderful support networks available today simply didn't exist back then, so parents had to put their ID children into state care (formal institutions) or manage themselves. With that said, we should never place any blame on any parent for relinquishing their disabled child to care, as that is not fair to those parents. We cannot possibly understand their unique plight.

I am sure that many who loved their child simply didn't have the emotional, practical or financial means to deal with the difficulties that arose every day. Be clear that I make absolutely no judgement about that; we all have different coping mechanisms or support systems. My decree with anyone dealing with any of life's difficulties is that we cannot fully understand how it must be for another's personal experiences, unless we have walked in their shoes.

Even so, I can well understand that to relinquish a baby would have been a heart-wrenching decision for many who had to place their child in one of the various state-run facilities. I have met parents who managed to care for their disabled child at home and reported they still felt the anguish of guilt every day, feeling responsible their child had to walk a difficult path in life. Many blamed themselves, thinking they had done something wrong.

There were others who did feel able to cope in a fashion, especially if both parents stayed to help raise the child. Once the babies grew and became more active, it was even more isolating for the mums, being home all day and often unable to go out. So some parents began to form babysitting play group support networks, offering a twofold benefit. Firstly, it gave the mothers respite from their isolation and an opportunity to tend to their other children. Also, their disabled child was able to start socialising with their peers without the ostracising glances so often presented in the wider community. That stigma is still evident today, so you can imagine how it was fifty or so years ago.

Another added benefit was that parents felt more understood and supported by the other parents as they could share advice on relevant matters. Thus began the early formation of 'self-help' groups, beginning as a form of shared child-minding then play groups so parents could have down time from their disabled child. Often disabled children lived in larger families, so attention was spread thinly between each member and extra support helped free up time for the parents — other siblings needed attention too and were often missing out.

The joy and sense of security was in knowing their little one was cared for by other parents who knew of the difficulties in raising a disabled child. Down syndrome, cerebral palsy and spina bifida are a few of the more identifiable disabling conditions, as these were more physically visible. But often, it was not clear what caused the disability, and the baby simply did not seem to meet the expected milestones of development and was fitted into the nebulous category of 'learning difficulty'. Today, these issues can be addressed by specialists, but not so well fifty years ago, so I raise my hat to those pioneers of childcare who did it tough.

The parents who developed that initial home-based 'play group' support network saw the numbers grow and, in time, it was clear they needed to find larger accommodation. This meant looking to community centres for space and hired rooms. As their children grew older it was hoped they could still learn different skills to cope with daily living, and parents needed to know if they could do more to improve their child's prospects.

These days we have 'special schools' that help families and their children with such disorders as autism, but in days gone by the options were not as great. All over Victoria, the formation of 'committees of management' evolved to formally lobby the government for greater assistance options for their growing children, as well as to administer the new day services that the government was willing to support financially. By far, the cost for staffing became the largest monetary consideration. Eventually, day training centres for their young adults began to expand across the country. No longer stuck at home, the growing numbers of children/adults had their own social outlets away from parents.

The next challenge for many of those aging parents was how their child would cope without them around, so they tentatively explored the different options of care and living accommodation, should they require it. Once the large institutions closed, smaller institutions came into place and provided supported care in a more home-friendly environment. Nevertheless, I interviewed several elderly parents over the years who were in grave need of assistance, yet reluctant to relinquish their beloved children to the new living systems. I could tell it was a heart-wrenching decision to make, but thankfully they realised it was the best choice and saw their child flourish.

I greatly respected their position, as over the many years, they struggled to care for their child on their own, and now relative strangers to disability (those employed as carers) were showing them a different way. It is important to appreciate what they had been dealing with for so long, and some elderly parents may refer to their adult son or daughter as if they were still a child. They managed a workable system to cope and that may have included an overprotective manner. It is not out of any need to control, but based on love and what they thought was the appropriate way to care for that loved child. For many parents, their son or daughter's age was merely a number and they considered their offspring a perpetual child.

Perhaps a young care worker, who has been taught they

must not assume their adult clients are children, finds it difficult to respect the 'old biddy' who cannot 'let go'. Be kind to these elderly parents and find ways around the differences in perspective of what you may think is best for your client, to ensure that everyone is feeling happy and valued. It can be the most difficult thing to have spent so long caring for their disabled child only to stand back to allow others to take over. It is wise to be insightful of cultural differences as well, as that can impact how one needs to adapt to changes. Please imagine how you might feel in the family's position, and then you may understand them a little better.

The best outcome I have seen from families finally making the decision to place a son or daughter into a residential facility is how relieved parents are to see their offspring settle in to their new abode. It might take much sensitivity from staff to convince parents they've made the right choice, and offering them to visit their disabled loved one can be useful. Even offering the prospective new resident some shorter initial visits can be helpful to all concerned. That way, questions can be covered and the parents can feel more familiar with the staff in the home.

I remember one elderly mother who had struggled on her own with her child far too long and went through this process over many months before finally conceding how wonderful it all was, saying, "I am so surprised at how well and quickly she has adjusted — should have been years sooner."

From my experience, family and friend visits are always encouraged. Sometimes, the client can go home for short stays or for special family events, and this only serves to enhance the quality of the new living arrangements for both parties. Open communication with family, if available and appropriate, can be an important part of helping a client feel more secure and move towards a measure of independence. Even a one-way conversation via the telephone can be enjoyed by someone who cannot speak. Their eyes light up at what the person on the other end is saying, so every contact has much relevance.

Likewise, family photo albums can be positive options to ensure family memories are reinforced. However, each individual's and family's position is unique and must be respected; staff opinions must never be forced. Your client is still their 'disabled child', though also understand that family contact may stir up unwanted emotions, so respect and caution must always be considered when encouraging connections between family members.

Interestingly, this adult/child issue raises the concept of 'age appropriate' options for activities. I once encountered a sticky situation when I was called to task over something I had done. This event occurred at the day facility of Robbie's 'Rainbow People', and while most there were ambulatory, there was a small group that often required assistance to manage different terrain or certain distances. On my first day at the centre, I was introduced to Rose, Mary, Ruth, Carol and Graham, who all had poor communication skills and appeared to have limited involvement in activities. I am sure they took in much more then they appeared to and every day their surrounding was a colourful hive of activity, with different groups moving from session to session.

I formed the impression, based on their lacklustre expressions and limited movement, that this small group was bored but could not say so. Sometimes their boredom led to unwanted behaviours, which I read as a cry for help for active or mental stimulation.

The first time I met them they were being 'herded' along together — I use this term as they presented as severely disabled, moving around awkwardly — and it seemed they were unintentionally made to be a spectacle in the community. My immediate impression was lasting and I felt we were doing them a disservice.

At the time, however, practicalities dictated that this 'lower functioning' group were placed together for security, often with just one staff attending. But these days, you can have two clients to one staff in public, which is a more dignified way to support your client with blending into the crowd.

But getting back to the 'situation'. It was a lovely sunny day and I had been outside with that group, trying to interest them in painting garden pots. It was a hands-on-hands affair (hands-on-hands refers to when a staff member has to put their hands on the client's to help generate the movement required, for example, using a paintbrush). The task seemed somewhat uninspiring to them, so I decided to take them on a bus ride to a local park to see some different scenery.

I thought I would still encourage some textural activities at the park by gathering interesting bits of nature to glue on the pots, such as bark, small pebbles, gum nuts and interesting leaves. I helped them onto the eight-seater bus and packed a folded wheelchair in case someone needed it. I wasn't going to stray more than a few metres from the bus at the park, and I took some refreshments along for a 'picnic' treat. That alone seemed to spur them to a measure of joyful spark. I started to get some eye contact as I spoke of where we were going and what we might do there. I remember using the word 'fun' quite a bit too.

Once at the park, we pulled up along the play area, as that was the most convenient place to park. Rose was off the bus first; she liked to sit on the ground so I sat her down nearby. It seemed that her self-designated task was to 'sort out' the bark on the ground into different sizes. Then came Mary, whom I seated next to Rose. Some pretty weeds nearby took her attention and she held on to a small bunch of yellow flowers she'd picked — who cared if they were crushed as the yellow was bright and happy.

Ruth started clapping her hands but became shaky when off the bus so I placed her in the wheelchair and moved her close to the other ladies. Carol precariously, but enthusiastically, walked to the monkey bars and enjoyed holding each bar, touching the round steel carefully. Finally, Graham, who walked on his tip toes and was looking around for any trains (his favourite of all sights to see), was last to alight. When I let go of his hand, he moved towards the swings. With the others watching, I helped him onto a swing and pushed gently as he held on tightly. He realised he could move himself with his long feet pushing a little higher with each slight kick. It seemed a revelation to him and he screamed with delight.

Well, that was it. Rose suddenly headed towards the second swing, and Ruth headed for a green frog spring rocker. She promptly pulled herself onto the seat and it started to wobble to her delight. Thankfully, the different play equipment seemed safe and included spring rockers, a seesaw, climbing bars and a low merry-go-round.

The next hour was spent in fun and frivolity. Everyone

had a go at something and there was much laughter. I loved seeing them come to life — something I'd never seen before.

As I watched them, I remembered a school play I was in as a child. I was meant to walk on stage to see my room after having returned from a holiday. It was a dark room and I had to turn on the light but I felt the audience's eyes on me, making me nervous. Suddenly everything changed when I hit the light. There in my play room I saw my toys had come to life, dancing and singing, and now I was watching the same thing as, in my mind's eye, the scene before me was a buzz of activity.

The park experience soon ended and we trundled back to the bus. The spell was broken and, as it turned out, I also seemed to have broken some rule that later had me facing a concerned and stern panel!

When we returned I naturally shared and explained how much my clients enjoyed their outing and, as far as I could tell, no one seemed to be against it. However, a week later I was asked to meet with the management team to discuss aspects of our park excursion. I was curious and puzzled, and I certainly never expected to have to justify the experience. Well, there I was being reprimanded for engaging my adult clients in 'non-age appropriate' activities. Up went my flag of injustice. I raised my hand to be the voice of my clients and ever so diplomatically declared how they might have related to their special outing.

"I saw them all living every minute of it, with eyes lit up, the large fixed smiles, the giggles, the hand clapping, the 'eh, eh, eh, eh' by one with tones of joyful laughter. It was the kind of response that I will promote whenever I can. It is called 'fun' and good for the soul. If you would like me to meet with the Committee of Management to describe how happily their son or daughter appeared during that magic hour of their lives, then please go ahead and arrange it. I welcome the opportunity to promote this kind of activity further. Otherwise, I will continue to do what I am doing with this group every week, in good weather, as that is what I *promised* them!" Then I walked out.

Well, I never did get to have that meeting with the committee and I kept the joy going. I noticed that group seemed brighter in general, so realised the positive feeling of having such fun transferred to other aspects of their lives. I believe that activity was even therapeutic, so I was quick to write it up in a report. Years later, it provided me with inspiration while offering advice to a friend who worked in a nursing home. She had been reprimanded for initiating an 'age-inappropriate' activity in the dementia ward. She had blown up different coloured balloons and invited some of the residents to toss them about.

My friend said the residents came alive, their eyes bright as they laughed and tried to hit the balloons — plus it provided them with exercise. It was hugely reminiscent of my experience with that little group in the park, so I decided to back up my advice and photocopied scientific papers substantiating how such activities with disabled or elderly residents were beneficial to their wellbeing and that we all, as adults at any age, can learn to have more fun. The studies recommended that even looking at children's books can be fruitful to help inspire our imagination — and how such pleasures help generate immune-boosting chemicals in our bodies.

Who would have thought that these days it is recommended to give high flying 'adult' corporate types a colouring-in book for a 'mindfulness' gift? It comes with the psychological recommendation of how this 'childish' activity is useful for freeing up one's self from the worry of yesterday, the anxiety of tomorrow and to bring us back to the moment of today. I daresay that my 'playground' group would concur with this and tell us something about learning how we all tick!

EIGHT

"There is no greater disability in society, than the inability to see a person as more"
— Robert M. Hensel

During the early part of my career in Canberra I worked with Tony, a middle-aged man who preferred to move about on the floor when home, as he felt it gave him greater freedom. Otherwise, he needed someone to push him in a wheelchair. Tony's thin limbs appeared twisted and distorted, with knotted fingers. His striking Greek appearance of thick black hair and dark eyes gave him a much-needed air of strength and determination. With his small lanky frame moving with a seemingly exhausting side shuffle along the floor, he managed to travel from room to room, and climb up and down from chairs and his bed. He was always very methodical about his routines and became frustrated when people forgot things, such as ordering his daily newspaper.

More than anything, he loved to read the *Canberra Times*, which was a large awkward-sized paper to manage, but he still turned the pages on his own with the attitude of a king. I had to curb my 'mother hen' self one day as I watched how he took five minutes to assemble the paper in the position of his liking. Each page was carefully scrutinised. The political, sport and general information was what he consumed, yet when he tried to share his ideas, the words came out all scrambled in stretched painful groans as he gasped for air through his partially blocked nose. Needless to say, this resulted in limited conversation. Yet, I saw before me a proud, intelligent and conservative man with positive self-esteem whom I respected, as did the other staff.

Years later, when discussing with others the need to respect one's personal dignity of self-worth, I once again thought of Tony and hoped he had been put in touch with some communication device that enabled him to share his thoughts. He was no one's fool, and he seemed to know instinctively if anyone was looking down on him. I recall once when a person visiting Tony's home had stared at him, and then left the room without speaking a word. Tony mumbled something to the effect of "I am a person" with a clear tone of indignation. I suspect it was not so much the stare that upset Tony, but that he was not acknowledged with something as simple as a polite hello or introduction. Yet I know that visitor meant no harm or disrespect.

Unfortunately, we allow appearances to help form our judgements of others — the quality of clothes, car, house, job — so imagine how a disabled person might feel about other people's perception of them.

As if matters of one's appearance weren't enough, I also saw how easy it was to make judgements about a person's behaviour or apparent motivations. My first example of this was when I began casual work as a student at a day facility in Canberra.

It came to my attention that a certain person I was assigned to work with was presenting some concerning behaviours. I visited there the day prior to starting work to meet the facility's supervisor, Allen. While talking with him, we heard a rather rowdy altercation in an adjoining room. Someone was clearly upset about where they wanted to be seated.

"Oh, that would be James. He has begun to display some aggressive manners in the last couple of months. He was fine when this place first opened, but now he seems to be troubled about something," said Allen thoughtfully.

"How long have you known him?" I asked, thinking James may be feeling homesick.

"Just since we opened, about five months, but he settled in well and for a time seemed happy with his new arrangements. He was polite, patient and certainly didn't present as an 'agro' character, and there was nothing in his file that indicated any aggressive tendencies, so this is puzzling."

"I presume you have explored all avenues for clues?" I asked, with my student research tone.

"Well, we have had meetings with all staff here, plus those at his day program in the community, and we've even been getting advice from a psychologist, but so far nothing."

"What about James, what does he have to say about his behaviour?"

"Well, that's probably the most frustrating part of all. He just seems to not want to discuss it. When we ask if he is unhappy about anything, or has any pain, he either shrugs his shoulders, says 'dunno' or walks away. Of course, we have had his medicals checked out with his doctor to see if he may be experiencing any pain or such, but no clues yet — we've even arranged a review by his psychiatrist," lamented Allen, as he handed me his file to read.

Then he added, "Even asking him about it now appears to

put him in a more agro mood too, and lately we have noticed this behaviour escalating. Like yesterday, he tried to push someone off the chair he likes to sit on. This is not fair to the other guys here either — they need to feel safe."

We, as students, had recently learned about the term 'challenging behaviour', and this was the first time I encountered such a situation. From what I could tell, James did not seem neglected in any way and, on the contrary, staff remained respectful and patient with him, going out of their way to try and help him. After meeting the other clients and staff, it seemed as though there were no personality clashes that may have potentially set him off.

My meeting with Allen ended, so we walked towards the dining room to see the young men standing around the table to be seated. Allen pointed to a red-haired man. "That's James. Can't miss him in a crowd, hey?"

Indeed so, I thought. I also noticed he was somewhat overweight and limped a little. His back was turned to me, and Allen called to him to turn around.

"Hello, James," I said with a smile. "I'll be coming here tomorrow to start working for a few months, but I can see you are about to eat dinner, so we can chat more when I'm on duty. But for now, I heard you like racing cars, so I was wondering if you are going to watch the Grand Prix this weekend?"

"Nah," was his only response, so I persisted.

"Well, when I'm on duty, I'll make sure it's on the TV in case you change your mind. Okay?"

"Yeah, okay" was an advance on no, so I quit while I was ahead and bid my farewell.

Upon my arrival for my first shift, I was pleased to see

James was watching the Grand Prix. Several hours later, as I was about to go home, I found James in the lounge room. "So how was your day, James, did you enjoy watching the racing cars?"

"Yeah, a bit," was barely whispered.

Hmm, I have graduated to at least three syllables in response, I thought, but I noticed he also seemed somewhat agitated as he was fidgeting with his belt and frowning. I decided to sit with him for a few minutes to share how my day was. I thought it better to push a 'problem' focus on me so he could hear that even staff have difficulties at times. Without him looking at me, I explained how my car tyre was flat so I was late for work, then how I broke my special cup as I hurried. I even deliberately sounded grumpy in sharing this.

James remained quiet as I rattled on with my story of frustration. I felt he was listening as he stopped fidgeting. When I was silent again, he spoke in a barely audible manner. "They make fun of me," were the few words that provided a potential clue to his troubles.

I did not wish to confront him with leading questions, so I only acknowledged his feelings. "Oh, I'm sorry, James, that must be very upsetting."

"I hate getting on the bus," was his next comment, still looking down at his feet.

We were interrupted when someone joined us, chatting and laughing at a joke on the TV: "Where do the sheep go to get their wool cut? At the BAA-BAAS."

This joke resulted in James chuckling and then walking off to retire in a happier mood. One joke I will not forget!

I conveyed what had happened with James to the supervisor, who, after a formal meeting, initiated a strategy to see what could be found out. James's weekly routine was to catch a bus each morning to his day program centre. A staff member James was not familiar with was assigned to covertly 'shadow' him on the bus. This 'observation' was needed only once.

It became apparent that James was subject to significant bullying from school boys who called rude things to him, and some deliberately kicked his legs and bag when passing him. The staff member reported that James seemed timid and quiet, but his face became almost as red as his hair. Presumably, he stored up his frustration and anger while being abused and threatened on the bus and released some of it once at home.

"Hey! You stupid fatty red head..." were words of a deeply personal description that James may well have felt too embarrassed to share — and a likely scene for an emotional pressure cooker scenario.

Everything made sense now about why James offloaded in a safer location. James's desire for privacy and secrecy was acknowledged and kept, but the use of a different bus was explored — one that did not have school children. This approach generated a welcomed outcome. And from that time, James reverted back to the gentle young man who seemed to enjoy his days. It would have been so easy to have gone down a different road. For it might have been concluded that he was in need of medication to make his behaviour manageable. Instead, it was found the 'environmental cue' provided an important remedy.

There was another situation that provided a startling example of not being aware of some environmental cue. I was at a meeting with a Behaviour Intervention Service

Team (BIST) who shared how they were called in to help find a solution for a young man named Tim, who had moved to a different residential home. There it became known that he loved to vacuum often and would spend ages doing it. The problem was that when he was finished, he would move away from the machine and start to scream/cry in a highly agitated manner.

While it was clear the situation was upsetting, no one wanted to take this vacuuming task away from Tim. Staff were perplexed as to the cause of his extreme outburst after he completed his much-loved activity. All kinds of suggestions were considered, but after many months his behaviour remained the same, until a casual staff member witnessed Tim's 'episode' and with keen observation asked, "Does Tim know how to turn off the vacuum cleaner?"

What a bombshell of insight, yet so completely simple. That was it, and as caring as everyone involved was, teaching Tim to turn off the vacuum cleaner was never even considered. The other relevant issue was that Tim did not know how to ask, and so was placed in that desperate situation. Once staff taught him how to turn off the vacuum, he would hit the switch and walk away proudly. The solution was right there in front of everyone. It took a new fresh observer to see it. With any behaviour of concern (BOC), please never give up and try to find the underlying cause. It may be something simple to you, yet significant to your client.

A new staff member to a facility might make a suggestion to have things function more efficiently, such as in the example above. I believe all suggestions should be welcomed. It is easy to take the same routine for granted, not realising there might be a better way of doing something. A fresh outlook need not be cause for feeling others are intruding on one's territory. I have seen how such resentments can erode a positive working relationship.

NINE

"The greatest barriers that persons with disabilities have to overcome are not steps or curbs, it's expectations"
— Karen Clay

The decree to not judge a book by its cover is a well-known one, and we know that covers come in many different colours. In the earlier years of my work with the disabled, I heard verbal labels such as 'loony', 'psycho', 'a nasty character' — and much worse — followed by 'alerts' in written reports. Because each report writer may have a different perspective on a given situation, the manner in which reports are written has evolved. This means the terminology is now carefully considered to reduce negative labelling. Reports are designed with respect to each client's privacy and dignity, and the information available is considered, as a protective element to all involved. In certain cases, a psychiatrist may be asked for advice when staff are faced with challenging behaviours, and the ongoing documentation provides a formal guide to determine the best form of assistance.

While clear explanations of a client's challenges need to be documented, derogatory terms should be avoided. The wording must relate to what happened in a given situation, and not include the personal attitude or feelings of the person making the report. For example, one cannot definitively say someone was 'happy' or 'angry' but only write a description of what was observed, such as 'he/she was smiling' or 'he/she was screaming'. This may seem counterintuitive, but such terminology is required in order to ensure that misinformation or personal judgements don't erode the accurate reporting of a given situation.

Any report can serve as formal documentation that guides another professional. If a psychiatrist becomes involved, those reports help determine what degree of chemical intervention, if any, may be necessary to help alleviate, reduce or eliminate negative emotions such as fear and anxiety that can cause challenging behaviours. It is not unusual for such individuals to take daily medications that address chemical imbalances so they can remain relatively anxiety free. Many of my clients experienced a dual or triple disability, which meant they were not only intellectually or physically disabled, but their medications were also under psychiatric supervision, generally with quarterly reviews.

The management of a client's BOC was often dealt with through 'restraint', which included 'time out' and medication. But over time, both were closely considered for their appropriateness to client wellbeing and these concerns gave rise to dramatic changes. Twenty plus years ago, a legacy of the institutional styles — the more custodial 'restraining' rooms — were still built into the smaller facilities. These special rooms were padded and sound-proofed. If one was to misbehave violently, then a visit to the 'time out' room was instigated. Thankfully, these rooms were eventually deemed unacceptable on many levels.

The second change happened over ten years ago, with psychiatric medication being deemed a potential chemical form of 'restraint'. However, in some cases, the pendulum of change swung too far. For example, the 'powers that be' took it upon themselves, without any formal agreement with staff or clients' doctors, to order such medications be reviewed (under supervision by medical professionals) with the request that "dosages be reduced" at least. This new rule impacted some clients negatively, and I will relate two that I knew about.

The first case regarded a young man, Tom, who had his medication reduced slightly. He presented as an active and enthusiastic personality and was keen to help with tasks, but he was prone to outbursts if he felt he was being reprimanded, as it hurt his pride. He did at times exhibit some learned negative behaviours and was selective as to how or when he presented them. But a simple intervention by staff to help explain things usually helped. When his medication was reduced, he became docile, lethargic and silent — appearing disconnected from those around him, not interested in his usual daily activities, and no longer communicating well. Overall, he seemed a completely different personality. It was a stark reminder of how much our chemistry can relate to our personality expression. Indeed, it was so drastic that when he was returned to his normal dose, just a tiny variation, we saw the same happy and enthusiastic Tom re-emerge.

The second client who was impacted by these medication changes was Joanne. She had been on carefully controlled psychiatric medication for many years. According to the old reports regarding Joanne's diagnosis of paranoid schizophrenia, her unique cocktail of medication worked appropriately and was not meant to be altered. Under that regime, she experienced a good quality of life. But this delicate balance was under grave threat as the formal decree of reducing her medication was made and, with the added concern that there may be a potential toxic overload with her usual medications, her psychiatrist, under duress, gradually reduced her medication over a year. The type of medication had to be changed as well due to a dosage-related issue.

I carefully documented Joanne's progress and, after a while, 'the voices' became more frequent and Joanne's physical health changed drastically. She looked like someone suffering from a severe flu and could not sleep. It took many phone calls to the facility's managers, Joanne's GP and family to try and help her, as well as dealing with the added problem of her previous psychiatrist retiring. I needed to find a sympathetic new one, which was not an easy task. During my research, I was told that in Australia, there is approximately one psychiatrist to every one hundred thousand people in the general population (but I stand to be corrected on that).

I eventually managed to find a psychiatrist who was even willing to make private visits to Joanne's home to supervise her condition closely. This was a good thing because her anxiety levels had escalated to a worrying degree, and with home visits she wasn't exposed to the stressful clinic waiting room environment.

Thankfully, it was decreed that Joanne have her previous medication reinstated but, unfortunately, given the nature of how those psychiatric medications work, the reversal had to be administered gradually over many months. In total, Joanne had to endure this upheaval for almost two years.

Naturally, the altering of medications was highly detrimental to Joanne's wellbeing and general health over that period of time. I am sure that in the institution days, many clients would have been given medication to render them 'zombies', but this new approach to combating 'chemical restraints' was not managed appropriately — and, in my view, constituted negligence.

I understand that long-term medications need to be monitored for toxic overload in the system, but my client's quality of life was seriously in question. She needed someone to help her tell those who had instigated the new medication policies how it was impacting her. It took time for my documentation of presenting behaviours to substantiate my plea and serve as evidence that something must be done in order to resonate with those policymakers.

I learned of the value of documentation over many experiences, so one must never underestimate their relevance and power to help make positive changes to a system that needs review. In the past I have been remiss in not documenting something by taking matters for granted and found that it let my client down when seeking a different approach as the change took longer. Documentation is stronger than any verbal report when it comes to seeking assistance for one's client. Never underestimate that process, but use it wisely.

Nevertheless, at that time of medication upheaval, and despite my endless documentation, I required the full support of Joanne's family who was worried about a potential toxic overload with her original medication. I eventually posed a serious question to them, along with the educated backing from Joanne's new psychiatrist. I presented two scenarios as a potential choice:

1. To have Joanne for ten happy years, during which time she felt well, slept well, enjoyed her social outlets, her friendships and daily routines, as well as continuing to enjoy her visits and family connections… even while risking a toxic overload (up until then, there was no evidence of any toxic overload).

2. Or to have Joanne for twenty years as emotionally and psychologically miserable, physically unwell, unable to sleep with ongoing and escalating anxieties and aberrant behaviours — including severe violent outbursts — all of which was already evident.

The family's response was immediate and the process of reverting back to the old medication regime began, leading to complete reinstatement of the old prescribed type and dosage. Joanne eventually returned to her former positive self. The first case I presented was short term and the second as with Joanne, long term, yet both cases were dramatic and finding that delicate balance of brain chemistry cannot be underestimated when decreeing new policies. Likewise, no two cases are the same and each case must be assessed on the basis of a huge range of potential variables and individual differences. In the disability field, it is never the case that 'one shoe fits all'.

A fine balance exists within the reporting system. For example, there are many circumstances where formal written reports may serve to ensure that everyone is on the same page, where something needs to be taken into close consideration to avoid potential upsets (as was Robbie's case with the missed alerts in relation to his cassette player). But reports can also generate negative expectations and even a degree of trepidation for new staff members towards their client, which in turn can impact on a client's emotions and cause the BOC to escalate.

So while reports are available for the overall wellbeing of the client, they also need to be approached with an open mind. Over the years, there have been occasions where I was verbally warned about a particular person's BOC in certain situations, then in reality found matters proved to be quite different when that person was presented with new expectations and approaches. I later saw how some written reports about clients reflected this warning as well.

One example occurred when I was to meet Jess after she arrived home from her day program. "Be careful of Jess. She is always aggressive if you don't give her a Coke when she comes home."

I ended up offering Jess a smoothie instead, which she willingly accepted. To be honest, I deliberately distracted her at the right time and she took the cue to try something different — and a much healthier option.

"Jess, I usually like to drink a fruity smoothie," I told her. "They're like a yummy ice-cream drink. Would you like to help me make one?" I asked casually. "I see you have great glasses on so you will be able to make sure all the bits go into the mixer."

She seemed to like what she saw as I put the smoothie together in a blender, and her task then was to pour the skim milk and yoghurt over the fruit. She especially loved being able to press the button to turn on the terrible sound. I had to convince her that one minute was quite sufficient!

After drinking it, however, she asked for a Coke so I told her if she had two drinks it might give her a tummy ache. Given the nature of the previous warnings, I was surprised how readily she accepted that explanation and I breathed a sigh of relief.

So we need to be mindful of how one individual's perspective, if shared as a 'must do', can change how others think about a situation or client. Mind you, it is not appropriate to dismiss a formal set protocol as it must be adhered to and appropriately changed after careful consultation with relevant parties. That is why formal meetings between staff and management are so important. While one needs to be discerning, they also need to take into account all aspects of a given situation. Most of all, everyone needs to be open to positive outcomes. It is a positive development that these days there is great focus and care used for the terminology written in reports. This can serve to maximise the client's position for appropriate support, as well as minimise staffs' potential to perceive a particular client in a negative light.

Another classic example of this concept of promoting 'expectations' occurred with a young lady named Kirsty, whose BOC reputation preceded her. The first time we were introduced, she presented a defensive stance and sported a cheeky grin. Her short light brown hair matched her top, which had a butterfly design on the front. In an effort to build rapport and trust, I told Kirsty that her shirt was very pretty and colourful and she asked me if I wanted to see her other tops.

Once in her room, she put her hand on my arm, moving her fingers in pinching position but not quite squeezing her fingers — yet. I had been told that she liked having power over staff by trying to intimidate them, thus giving her a reputation as a 'nasty type'. With a determined but friendly tone to my voice, I looked directly at her face and asked, "So, Kirsty, I believe you are a nice young lady, and not a little naughty child, is that right?"

Her hand was still poised to pinch but I chose to ignore that.

She stared at me with a surprised look as if she was rather thrown by my question. "I-I-yeeees," was all she could manage.

"Well, I knew that because you look like a nice polite lady," I said convincingly, overlooking the mischievous expression on her face. She dropped her hand and focussed on removing some tops from her wardrobe for me to take a look at. After her clothes display, to my many compliments, she carefully put them away.

I left her to it so I could chat to the staff in the next room. They informed me, amongst other 'do's and 'do not's, to never take Kirsty to the shops as she becomes violent and destructive there. I later read some serious events related to such behaviour and it wasn't pretty.

"She screams loudly, pulls items from shelves and runs amok, so never take her out. When in that state, she refuses to listen to reason. Also, we have a duty to the public, as it frightens them," I was told.

I didn't underestimate the awful experiences of previous shopping events, and I understood why they would want to warn me, but I wondered if there was another way, another opportunity for Kirsty to experience a positive shopping outing.

Well, I got to know Kirsty well over a few weeks and it became clear to me that she loved the idea of saving money to buy herself something and wanted to own a pink top. She was given a small fortnightly allowance and it was agreed to be used as positive motivation for a shop purchase, with a staff member purchasing the item. This seemed a worthy target for enabling her to express herself in a more positive manner — one that gave her a sense of pride — to experience some praise. So the next week, I offered her a proposal: "Now, Kirsty, I've heard that you have not behaved well in the past in shops, but I believe you *can* behave well there as you did say you are not a naughty child and are a lady. Is that right?"

"Yes," she said in a less defensive, and even curious, tone. But I could tell she was processing that notion too. She stood there for a few seconds, with her somewhat startled look, then added, "I-I-I'll be good."

"Well, yes, I think you *can* be a perfect lady while shopping too, and I am prepared to take you *just once*, to give you a chance to prove to me you can do it."

This time with her focus on me, she appeared more relaxed, so I outlined how the shopping expedition would go.

"So, Kirsty, if you behave well at the shops, we can look for a nice top that you can choose and pay for yourself." After a pause to enable her to digest that, I added, "Then if you do that well, after we finish our shopping, we can even have a treat at a café."

She seemed to realise this was all a possibility so responded with, "I love coffee and doughnuts."

"Okay, but now listen carefully. If you don't behave — even just a tiny bit — or you complain about anything at all, we will leave the shops and immediately come back." I paused for few seconds, then said, "So, if you behave like a naughty child at the shops, I will never ever take you out again." I went on to say that this was a great chance to show me how she was a lovely lady, to which she again promised to behave. It was a deal.

I could tell she knew from my facial expression and tone of voice that I meant what I said. Kirsty began smiling and agreed to my terms, so we started making a plan. "Let's look to see how much money you have saved and when you get to twenty-five dollars we can arrange an outing. Just us girls, okay?" I said as she hurried to show me her money box.

This was an entirely different approach to how she managed the whole shopping idea. By planning to purchase a special top with her own money, then selecting something, this meant she needed to own the task and take some responsibility for her behaviour. That was most important. Given she was so motivated to engage in this type of activity, I saw how this could enable her to demonstrate what she was capable of, and a way to show her 'full potential', which was a term so often written but not always fully understood.

The shopping trip was a resounding fun success in every way, and Kirsty was so proud of herself. To be honest, during that first outing, I had forgotten about the previous warnings, as we were both so involved in searching for the right shop. We went shopping many times more, during which occasions Kirsty never once faltered. I praised her often for her good behaviour and told other staff, "Kirsty was such a lovely lady in the shops, always polite and patient" to help reinforce this new belief of herself.

I found that this shared experience had a follow-on impact in other areas of her life. For example, Kirsty seemed to be more confident in how she behaved around others; it was as if she discovered this lovely young lady within her whom she seemed to rather like. When expressing this part of her identity, she was helpful, cooperative and calm. However, I found Kirsty was more prone to become negative when she felt bored, so providing more stimulating activities helped kerb her tendency to get attention from others by disturbing them. It meant being constantly vigilant.

The second benefit to Kirsty's success at the shops was that she seemed to appreciate that I believed in her and gave her a chance to do something she had previously ruined. Obviously, having a positive working relationship with others meant she was able to demonstrate her new-found confidence often. When I saw her last, she was telling people that she liked to go shopping, and her psychiatric medication was not needing a follow-up PRN (*Pro re nata*: 'as needed') as often.

Another occasion when I was warned about a potential client's BOC related to a thirty-five year old man named Gary. I was warned, "He can demonstrate very abusive tendencies, both verbally and physically, especially towards female staff, so be careful."

As a rule, I preferred to visit someone prior to working with them. I felt it was a courtesy and enabled clients to feel less threatened when they saw me again. As I did with Kirsty, I always found something to personalise about the client that would help set the scene for future experiences.

So there I was, standing in the lounge. I saw Gary watching a loud grating rock concert video. Thankfully, another staff turned it down.

"Come over here please, Gary, and say hello to Barbara. She has agreed to come and work here with you."

Gary's blond hair seemed well gelled to a spike in the middle and he was dressed in matching pale green pants, shirt and sneakers. About my height, Gary stood a metre from me with arms tightly folded and a look of suspicion. I moved forward and extended my open hand towards his, and he returned a loose clammy grip as he turned towards the TV again. It was clear to me that he felt anxious. I knew this type of trepidation when a client was faced with uncertainty, and it was something new staff can underestimate — so a friendly approach can help.

"I do like the green sneakers you're wearing, Gary. I bet those rockers would love to have them too."

With that, Gary seemed to relax a little and made quick glances between myself and the TV.

"Yes, I start tomorrow, and I believe that you are a polite and helpful gentleman so maybe you can help me find my way around here," I stated confidently, while noticing his surprised expression.

I also knew that he loved his cuppa because there was an issue about him demanding a coffee too often, but I was not about to change his routine of having one at set times. I was told that "caffeine sets him off" — so many battles were fought over how often he drank it, leading staff to create a coffee schedule for him.

"We can start with you showing me where the kettle and mugs are as I like my cuppa too. How about that, Gary?" I asked, by now having gained his full attention.

"Good," said he with a half grin, while walking back to sit on the couch, but also glancing back at me as I spoke to the other staff for a few more minutes before waving goodbye with a smile.

For the next two years, I can honestly say that at no time did Gary once present as anything but a gentleman towards me. He was indeed helpful and always seemed to accept my reasoning about issues, such as how he wanted too many coffees and how he procrastinated tidying up after himself.

Yet, Gary certainly understood I was fair and attentive towards his needs, and we seemed to have a mutual respect. Mind you, I did see how he was quick to express his 'abusive tendencies' towards certain peers or the occasional staff, but he was careful to never direct it towards me. I felt sure he did not want to erode what he considered my positive view of him. But he almost did once, then I watched his hurried self-correction. I found that interesting, in that he had apparent control over what was presumably 'spontaneous' BOC.

With witnessing these different sides of Gary's behaviour, I felt as though he was living up to my expectations of him, but he needed to let out any frustrations or anxieties towards others. I suspected this aggressive display was more of a subconscious strategy or defence mechanism towards some kind of perceived threat. Yet I could well imagine how it might have been living in a large institution of mixed types, with limited security, feeling the need to protect oneself if someone nearby was in an aggressive mood.

This theme of violent outbursts linked to feelings of anxiety was evident with another lovely lady called Renee. She loved nothing more than to look like a film star. Her thick naturally wavy hair framed her facial features in a way that transformed her into a beauty with just a 'bit of lippy'. Simple things gave her much pleasure, such as having privacy for her personal items and being able to have her own room, which she kept neat and tidy.

Renee liked to take her own 'time out' in her sanctuary of soft toy animals, floral paintings and well-dressed dolls. Imagine how it must have been for Renee to share a room with others when she had lived in a dormitory years earlier. How easily we take such matters for granted. I read archived reports about the institutions and ascertained that that type of shared accommodation was not conducive to emotional stability.

Thankfully, due to the closure of the larger institutions, Renee was able to move into a smaller place that enabled all residents to have their own room. She was another of my clients diagnosed with paranoid schizophrenia, which was largely controlled by daily medication, yet at intermittent times she would report 'the voices'. I noticed that any dramatic variation to her emotions, positive or negative, could trigger anxiety, leaving her in a disturbed state. At times it happened out of the blue when all seemed relaxed. I often considered that her disturbed state may have been caused by internal triggers based on confused thoughts or memories. It was never clear if the anxiety or 'the voices' came first, but Renee reported them when she appeared stressed about anything, real or perceived.

There were times when external experiences were the cause of her anxiety. For example, Renee was found to become angry and threatening with new staff. I considered that, given her precise daily routine was so important to her, she worried new staff would not know specific things about her routine.

Even though every client's personal profile was well documented and relevant information was readily available to all staff, evidently Renee did not feel she could rely on new staff reading that, so her anxiety when faced with a new staff member rose dramatically, leading to aggressive outbursts. Unfortunately, it was not always practical for Renee to be alerted to impending changes, and there was still that issue of trust. I saw this once when I was telling her of a new staff member coming, she acknowledged it, but while turning to walk away from her I heard her mumble something quietly. "Do I like porridge?" This was an issue she evidently hoped the new staff member would know about her, as she hated porridge.

I decided to write a one-page chart of the specific details she needed staff to know and pinned it on her door, where new staff would easily see it. I asked Renee what she wanted staff to know about her and read it out to her once I was finished. That seemed to reassure her, and subsequent reports suggested she behaved more relaxed when in the presence of new staff.

Putting that chart up, with Renee knowing what was written on it, was a simple visual reminder and reassuring strategy, but one that could have easily been overlooked. I relate and emphasise this story as it demonstrates how useful it can be to pay close attention to the more unique needs of any client. It is that uniqueness that so often gets lost when working with many individuals in a busy and stressful environment. So I repeat, it can never be a case of 'one size fits all' with any group.

TEN

"The worst thing about disability is that they see it before they see you"
— Easter Seals

It is not difficult to grasp the repercussions of antagonistic personalities being paired. I refer to situations where some outwardly rebellious clients were assigned staff with a dominant personality to manage them. In these instances, fear and violence will often be the outcome. Psychologically speaking, we are all capable of developing our identity purely based on the role models in our environment. One can imagine how that culture of dominance could foster further tensions and, as such, some of the clients may exhibit a form of learned aggression.

I was told of one such instance that occurred at a large institution, where a young man who could not speak refused to eat and screamed when a staff member began spoon-feeding him breakfast. As punishment, he was not given any more food that day.

How might that young man have felt? Perhaps he felt unwell and, as he couldn't speak, he screamed. He became feared and treated as a violent person in need of punishment. How would any person feel, let alone a disabled one who cannot speak or defend themselves, from such total disrespect? How could a sense of trust towards anyone evolve in them? Can you imagine being unable to move and left to sit all day in a large cold room with nothing to do and no one to help clean you after having a 'toilet accident'? You then, along with others in the same situation, get taken to a concrete courtyard in a naked state to be hosed down with cold water.

Over the years, I have heard many more stories like this one and have seen firsthand the outcome of those who were mistreated. Once released from those institutions, they often resorted to violent outbursts, giving the impression they were violent people. Perhaps these individuals, after being threatened or ignored, learned to express their private pain and frustration through desperate means. Perhaps others may have only been able express the dreadful, lonely silent scream while rocking for hours, occasionally moaning. I witnessed that in my early student days when visiting the Kenmore Institution. I don't discount that there were staff in those archaic institutions who were insightful and caring, as I have met some personally. However, they were not always on duty and the staff-to-client ratio was inadequate to ensure appropriate individual care.

Thankfully, on one auspicious day, I heard several positive speeches that suggested the tide was finally turning for the better. I was invited to attend the formal closure of a major institution in Melbourne in the early 1990s. A range of guests provided visual displays and accolades of how different life was to become for the former residents, as well as stories of the sad existence experienced by several individuals in that place. But more than anything else, what has mostly remained in my memory of that day is the huge, beautifully bound book showing the names of former residents with the reason for their entry. I believe it was only one of many volumes. But this one was enough to embrace the culture of attitude that prevailed during those early days of operation. I noted the brilliant handwriting and the overall artwork of this large record and how it seemed in direct contrast to its contents.

One entry referred to a young orphan, Missy, whose parents had been killed in a car accident. Missy was only eight when her aging aunt brought her to the institution. I could imagine that child may well have been traumatised and in a disturbed emotional state over her loss. Maybe she became too challenging to manage, especially for the old lady who left Missy in the institution for the rest of her life. How did Missy see her world, which had crashed down on someone so young? I often thought of that little girl as an example of so many other young people who found themselves in a strange place with no personal attention. I wondered how they managed to relate to their world.

During the speeches that day, someone told a story of a young brother and sister. They were placed in separate 'gender' wards, never to know how close they were to each other until they became adults. A staff member who had worked in both wards, which were separated only by a thick locked door, noticed the unusual surname and investigated if they might be related. Just like that, they found each other and the only consolation was that they were not separated again, remaining together until their deaths several years later. Too late for blame, but did anyone ever say sorry to them?

I once worked with a lovely lady, Nora, who was separated

from her eleven siblings when her mother died and her father was unable to cope. At age twelve she and her siblings were placed into care but Nora never had contact with them again. I would have assessed her as a moderately capable person in the ID rating scale, but she still required permanent supervision for her safety and care. She was a sweet-natured lady who never seemed to be anything but appreciative of how well she was being looked after. Such a disposition in the large institution would have meant she was never focussed on too much or in need of some tougher minded staff to control her.

Yet she did privately confess how sorry she was that she lost touch with her 'people'. Thankfully, from her own assessment, she led a comfortable, safe and joyful life for more than seventy years in care.

Once placed in the suburbs, former residents of the Melbourne institution were offered their own room, giving them more privacy, peace and respite from the constant range of people around them. Each new home still had to be shared with four other individuals, with no say in who they may be. The compatibility factor was highly regarded when considering the placement of individuals, but mistakes were made.

To be fair, given the complexities of the newly formed structures and ongoing financial constraints, decisions were made in good faith, while having in mind the wellbeing of the client. I don't underestimate the pressures those decision makers were under, as that evolution of change for new accommodation for the disabled happened so rapidly during the early eighties. Even the staffing of policymakers and carers handling numerous changes was dynamic and unpredictable.

The accommodation issue was the largest consideration as new benchmarks were being set. It is now standard for each home to have 24/7 supervision with a 5:2 client-to-staff ratio — a vast improvement over the old style of 30:2 ratio. Having such an improved living policy meant many doors opened up for those new residents. It was such a different way of doing things for the disabled, but as I said, many unsung heroes who provided a strong clear voice for the disabled pushed for countless years to make it all happen.

From my observations over the past thirty-odd years, the ruling governments have been instrumental in a whole new industry of care towards the disabled. The dramatic changes created a rapid learning curve for many dedicated people. But like anything new and different, mistakes were made, but not for want of many professionals working tirelessly towards a positive outcome for all. They had to grasp a better understanding of the human condition in order to manage this transition with cost-effective mandates.

Mind you, my more cynical side was suspicious about the government's overall motivation for such drastic changes. After all, these large institutions on parcels of acreage were placed away from the general population (which eventually changed as new developments in housing opened up, moving closer to the institutions), so the closure of the institutions provided the 'powers that be' with some valuable real estate opportunities. Nevertheless, the extra funds could to go towards implementing many proposed changes for the disabled and doubtless, many did seek the changes for humanitarian reasons, and that highly desired outcome is all that matters now.

Thankfully, there are many who understand the need for greater respect and acceptance of anyone who may seem different. I understood this when I took the role as coordinator for one of seven Outreach Pilot Programs being set up in and around Melbourne. This new initiative was in response to the 'spilling out' of ex-residents from institutions. For each of the seven Outreach bases, the task, essentially, was to help a group of five individuals from one of the new residential homes.

This was a revolutionary approach to caring for the disabled, and I walked towards it all with great expectations. But first I had to deal with my own prejudices, which surfaced when I was given the five new individuals' paperwork, with a brief that stated I must "spend the first six months to get them to feel confident enough to move from their house to their front gate". Having no idea what that might entail, I decided to keep an open mind — 'keep going with the flowing' became my mantra.

Of course, the overall aim was to eventually integrate those five individuals into the wider community and to ensure they had maximum — yet appropriate — exposure to many different types of experiences. Unfortunately, within each individual's profile there was a section titled 'Challenging Behaviours', and it was all blanked out — most being several pages long! Added to these blanked out pages, there were black-and-white photocopies of black-and-white photos, resulting in the five individuals assigned to me appearing rather dubious-looking, with the impression they may even have violent tendencies.

I forged ahead and soon met them. I felt ashamed I had so easily made false assumptions about them, and admonished myself many times for jumping to conclusions prior to meeting my new clients. I now realise how easy it is to assume things based on what may be pre-empted in both written and verbal form.

But back then, these first five clients were my examples of hope and optimism. They were lovely natured and patient. In fact, by their demonstration of enthusiasm, I had this image of birds being let out of a cage, keen to fly. I forgot about the report I'd been shown, which suggested it may take six months for them to find their confidence, as it only took a week to get them out in the community and learn their needs, wants, preferences and, above all, what made them laugh.

Amongst those five was a middle-aged couple, Billy and Suzie, who had known each other for many years back in the institution and had formed a close bond. Suzie was a gentle, softly spoken and dignified lady who enjoyed attending church weekly. She also loved to draw, often using a whole pack of marker pens in one sitting. Her childlike images showed friendly scenes of people, animals and flowers, all coloured with love and joy.

Being rather shy, Suzie would giggle when she was complimented for her artistic work, and I could see how this lady may have looked as a young girl — who surely would have been lovely to have around. So why did she spend so many years in a large institution? When asked how Suzie liked this new place, she clasped her hands in prayer position and seemed to hesitate, carefully considering before declaring, "This is my bestest place ever where me and my poor Billy ever lived."

The new supervisor of that house was admirable, as were the regular staff, and it soon became obvious the 'famous five' were being treated like royalty. With their lovely bedrooms, fun activities, nutritious and delicious meals, and thoughtful adherence to health and medication, it must have seemed like a fantasy. Each of their bedrooms were lovingly decorated with personal items — one very pretty with soft toys and paintings of flowers, another with ceramic ornaments and a colourful bedspread, another with footy memorabilia.

Another one of the five was Bettina, a middle-aged lady whose 'holy place' was any op-shop. There she would happily sift through little trinkets to offer as 'thank yous' to whoever was kind to her. Once she found a booklet on friendship and she liked me to read it to her over and over again. A prize find was a cassette of the singers Foster and Allen, and I am sure it wore out completely. It was a standing joke how she was able to buy and donate back to the op-shop 'similar' looking items over different weeks. But above anything, she loved to give.

Another resident was Frank, who looked like a fighter with his rough features and many missing teeth. He was a lovely gentle man of few words who tended to stand around with his arms folded and appeared anxious with too much attention. He preferred to hold back and observe keenly, and find his own way to communicate and participate. One time when he was proudly helping me carry goods to the car at the local shops, we heard a man's gruff voice call out from behind us. "G'day, ye old bastard!" said the man with much enthusiasm and a display of wildly waving arms.

Everything happened so quickly, as the man seemed in a hurry, so after a short stop to tell Frank he was looking great, the man beckoned farewell and vanished out of sight. I assumed he was a past resident but Frank could not tell me how he knew him. I did question, but I only received a "Yeah" from Frank to all queries, which did not clear up the man's identity. It didn't seem to matter though, as that encounter absolutely made his day and Frank kept repeating his mysterious friend's Aussie 'term of endearment' many times over to others, with a big smile — hastily followed by my explanation!

Frank wore that look of feeling very special. A link to a personal friendship perhaps? Such is the puzzle of those who cannot share their more complex thoughts. But thankfully, his new friendship base grew and that was gratifying to see, as he seemed content and happy accepting new contacts and indulgences.

Those four clients were somewhat older than the final male resident, Jake, who was a ball of energy in his early twenties. While he remained patient, it was clear the older age mix was not the best match for his energy level, personality and future learning — one of those compatibility errors I spoke of earlier. Thankfully, he was later relocated to another residence with a younger set, with more appropriate interests and activities. However, for a couple of years, Jake participated in the Outreach program, ever keen to experience and explore further community options.

I found Jake loved to visit the Kevin Heinze Garden Centre in Melbourne — a place donated by Mr Heinze for the benefit of the disabled — and engage in different weekly projects. Disabled groups were assigned to rostered times for one or two hours. Different groups of all ages and genders attended, as well as students from nearby schools who wanted to engage in work experience.

There were also rostered volunteers there at all times to guide the disabled in their varied tasks, such as potting soil, planting seedlings and, on rainy days, making cards with a nature design. It was a constant hive of activity that everyone seemed to enjoy immensely. One middle-aged man loved nothing more than to fill a wheelbarrow full of soil or mulch and take it to different locations. I think the mechanics of his 'one wheeled machine' intrigued him more than anything else. I used to envision him as a landscape gardener, under different life circumstances. Then the busy activities concluded with the ubiquitous Aussie treat — the 'cuppa and bickie' break!

One time, Kevin Heinze decided to run a competition for the best miniature garden design, so I suggested to Jake that we build one. Well, he nearly jumped out of his skin and agreed by repeating, "Ya ya — ha ha!" He fully focused on the project. A cardboard box provided the base for a garden design that depicted a small village. Jake loved to handle the pieces that formed the hut. He glued the grass on and placed the soil, bark, plants and animals strategically. I was not sure of the little pig sitting on the hut, however, so I told him that he must be the only person who thought pigs can fly! I got lots of laughter over that and never knew how he got the joke. A good example of how we can underestimate anyone. But best of all was a little plastic person I named Jake. When he was choosing a place to put it, he was very quiet and serious. Such a special moment to observe.

So did his 'village garden' win? Well, while ours looked 'ok-ish', there were others that were more impressive. But Mr Heinze, who judged that day, privately told me Jake's moved him emotionally the most. It won on the perfect merit of filling Mr Heinze's private brief. Jake took that small trophy home so proudly. I doubt a gold medal Olympian could have felt prouder than Jake as he gleefully showed it to everyone!

I learnt from those seven years of Outreach that while there definitely is a need for certain relevant information to be documented and shared, taking people on face value remained my motto for everyone I worked with, and it served me well over many years.

This small group of intellectually disabled individuals taught me a lot about not allowing the past to dictate the future. I am sure that each one of them made the most of every situation. Their new world offered privacy, a quiet space and variety of life, when previously they had been denied much of that. But they were each able to face new challenges with enthusiasm and gratitude, taking nothing for granted. It speaks volumes of the human spirit. This newly formed family became living proof of a "worthwhile quality of life" after the formal closure of the institutions.

I saw many different residential homes over the years, and all of them seemed to provide exceptional facilities and conditions for their new residents. But over time, beyond the aesthetics and conditions of the house, I found the single most important factor for generating a positive living experience for any client, in any situation, was all about personalities and, more specifically, the quality of staff.

Eleven

"When you read the word disability, see 'possibility'"
– Unknown

In earlier days, during the spill out of the institutions, it was possible for someone with no formal training in human services to enter the disability field. Mind you, training and formal qualifications does not guarantee a person will have the right attributes to be associated with disabled people, and some of the best workers have started with no relevant formal qualifications. During the early years of my career, some of the best people who cared for the disabled were ex-domestic workers from the institutions, and ordinary mums and dads who had dealt with the many complexities of supporting families. At times when I have had young students working around me, I could tell within five minutes if they were appropriate to work with the disabled. It was nothing to do with how well they performed, or even if they were qualified. It was simply the way they related to the clients.

On the flip side, I once met a highly-qualified worker in the field whose personality was unsuitable for working with the disabled or carers, with her treating both groups as if they were beneath her. Being academically accomplished and able to recite the 'holy grail' policy does not ensure a person knows how to relate to client or staff. There are times when people make decisions about clients that are not in their best interests, and it is these times when I have stood up for my clients, never giving up on trying to find a way around a potential conflict between myself and policy dictates.

I did not see the need to win friends or score 'brownie points' within the establishment, but merely to ensure my client's voice was heard, especially when they were unable to express it themselves. I felt the need to be a front-line advocate to their needs.

Regretfully, I have known some questionable characters employed in the field too, so today, to ensure potential staff have the proper credentials, all are subject to strict adherence to policy via formal standards with specific certification and training. Many may consider that only dedicated people are drawn to working with the disabled, and I have spoken to some who retired early from other higher status jobs because they felt the need to redefine their personal sense of value. But sadly, in every field there are 'bad apples' who will use their position to exploit the vulnerable, and the disabled are often easy targets for control and manipulation. Unfortunately, not everyone employed in the disability field is worthy of their role.

This issue reminds me of an event that happened many years ago. I was helping several of my clients purchase drinks. For some clients, it was a hands-on-hands affair, with me having to help them remove their wallets, collect the money and place it on the counter. Even with my help, those clients were still able to feel they owned some measure of purchasing their drink 'independently'.

As we proceeded, the well-meaning shopkeeper offered

to provide the drinks for free and, while I appreciated the gesture, I explained the specific learning program for my clients and he said he understood. But then he followed with, "Oh, you must be such an angel to work with these people," in an admiring tone.

"Not necessarily," I snapped, even surprising myself, then hastened to add, "There are some people in this field who are bullies and treat their clients with gross disrespect, as they intimidate, dominate and even physically abuse them."

I was fresh from dealing with a grave concern I had regarding a certain staff member's behaviour towards her clients. I had to take the grievance through an eleven-step process, which invariably involved the police. After weeks of interviews and paperwork, I was informed by a very regretful police officer that there was nothing they could do as the only witness was the client and her statement would not be admissible in court as evidence. The perpetrator of the abuse, which left the client with bruises (which I photographed and had the doctor verify) was merely shunted around the system. This was not uncommon to merely shuffle those 'bad eggs' sideways to resurface elsewhere in a position of 'care'.

Any potential grievance begins with a formal Incident Report, which are serious documents that must be followed through by all relevant parties; this process forms an important protective element to those who aren't able to speak for themselves. But so often, clients still remained at risk. These days, any grievance that involves harm towards a client results in instant dismissal with questions asked later. The system is now so finely tuned that false accusations or misinformation could result in innocent staff being harmed, and even dismissed, but at least it serves notice to all staff to be on alert about their performance on all levels — act appropriately and there is nothing to worry about.

I remain on the side of pessimism about the NDIS system if it remains that a client's evidence cannot be admissible in court. That can feel heartbreaking for a harmed client and their family. If this issue is not addressed, many more disabled individuals may be subject to abuse. The answer is to ensure clients are fully protected at all times, while considering a client's right to privacy.

Surely, if there is any suspicion that a client is being harmed, installing CCTV cameras may offer a deterrent to continued abuse. Likewise, staff who report such incidents must be protected from the threat of dismissal by those who'd prefer to keep things covered up. Otherwise, the system will be seen as a cost-effective measure only, and all the good work of those who poured their hearts into the project with their recommendations may well be denigrated for their assumed negligence.

But back to my sharp comment to the kindly shopkeeper. I quickly explained that while any place of work can have some questionable characters, I emphasised that the majority of workers in the disability field are decent, caring individuals who work diligently to help their clients. As we were leaving, he said he still thought I had wings, so I told him, "Okay, I'll wear my 'crushed wings' next time I'm here," as a joke, and thankfully I left with us both laughing.

It is normal for any worker to feel burdened by their own difficulties, and may even need counselling to work appropriately with those in their care. Good managers are alert to this and hence, over time, more and more emphasis has been put on ensuring staff are supported, so there is a professional approach to employing staff appropriate to the task. We are all human and it is not always easy to deal with stressful situations, but I have found certain managers tend to behave as if staff must function independently of emotions. There seems an element of disrespect in that.

I see nothing wrong if workers share private issues with other staff during breaks, as it can relieve some pressure and foster a supportive environment. This can help them deal with the business of their day more freely. Team support in this field is a positive, especially when being confronted with clients' BOCs, as stressful interactions between all concerned can make for a disharmonious environment. Policymakers will do well to remember that carers are not robots.

This also means if a staff member feels unable to cope in any given situation that may lead to a client's wellbeing being compromised, or if they feel unable to offer their best to that client, then the staff member must either seek help or request a transfer.

For any staff who feel they are not coping in a specific environment, it is important to look at the avenues available to address that. It is not a matter of avoidance but of being professional and honest. No one should be ostracised in any way for that, and I personally see it as a strength for one to recognise their 'personal limitations' in order to find a positive outcome for all. I know that workers do get support when it is requested, and the system has a process set up for this. But feeling unhappy and complaining is not going to change anything for the better. Action is required until a solution can be found.

I experienced a stressful situation several years ago when

it came to my attention that a certain defenceless blind lady, Kym, had another client vent her frustration on Kym's head. It was clear this was an extremely incompatible placement and very dangerous, if not hugely upsetting to Kym. I was shocked and made it my business to question and complain about this deplorable situation. Despite being told that only the chief supervisor could make a decision on the matter, I felt Kym — who was unable to speak up for herself — needed this extra support.

Basically, I defended that client's right to feel safe and secure in her own home — which was set down in policy anyway — so I relentlessly approached the appropriate parties until something was done about it. I actually stormed into the chief's office and explained how unacceptable the situation was, spelling out some salient facts. He glared at me as he sat taller in his chair for a moment and asked in a stern voice, "Are you trying to tell me how to do my job?"

"Well, if you keep that client in that dangerous situation any longer, yes, I suppose I am doing just that," I replied with an equally official tone.

He went on to note I did not work in that particular client's area and had no right to intrude. So I said, "I feel that no matter where I work, all the clients under my radar are my responsibility. It is my job to be a voice for them if they are in trouble and nothing else is being done — this has gone on for too long as it is."

With that, he slumped back on his chair and in a quiet, more reflective tone, he said, "You know, my father always said that if there is evil in the land and no one does anything, then nothing will change."

I thanked him for his time and left. I simply couldn't give

up until changes were made and I never blamed the offending client. She was also in need of an appropriate placement as numerous personal factors dictated how she managed her frustrations on vulnerable targets. Kym was shortly moved to another home.

Mistakes can easily be made by anyone with good intentions, but there is no excuse for failure through ignorance of facts if they are available. In this field, the whole notion of confidentiality means that important facts — the ones that relate directly to a client's wellbeing — may not be made available. At times, confidentiality can be a double-edged sword: too much information can result in setting up negative expectations, but it is equally relevant to know what to specifically avoid as a known trigger for preventing upsetting a client.

Many years ago, a new client had arrived without anyone having access to his formal reports. The notion of confidentiality had gone to that extreme. So no one knew how imperative it was to never say "no" to him in any context. One day, soon after arrival, he was being shown something during an art class and the word "no" was used in an innocent way. He suddenly screamed and became extremely upset. Naturally, this spoiled the art experience for all but, more significantly, it left the client emotionally 'tangled' for the rest of the day.

To draw the line on which information should be confidential and what should be disclosed can be tricky, but common sense must prevail in all cases. Likewise, all reports may have variations to it from each individual perspective, so it may even depend on the perspective of who is writing the report. Conflicts may well be recorded, but I have found too many times where new opportunities have overridden older circumstantial evidence across new situations. The Duty of Care formulae dictates adherence to certain rules, but my take also involves the notion that each day is a new day, each individual is unique and one must presume all positive expectations.

I often didn't focus on any disability in my clients, as their intrinsic selves — the part that determines we are all equal — was always evident. That's not to say they didn't require my assistance or that their differences did not exist, but more that they demonstrated just how similar they were to me. Most of the hundreds of clients I met over the years were essentially no different to anyone else I knew in my life.

Regardless of whether we present some form of disability, everyone is born with a certain 'nature' and personality predisposition, but our environment — our life experiences and the 'nurture' part — can dictate their expression. Also, anyone, regardless of the severity of their disability, feels the full range of emotions. I say so based on a disturbing conversation I had many years ago with a parent who obviously loved her son dearly. Although he was heading for age fifty, she saw him as a child.

I had come to know this man, Michael, very well. He had a quiet personality with little conversational ability. He still managed to convey his feelings such as love, anger, pride, joy, disappointment, etc — all these emotions were obvious within just one of his life experiences, where he saw himself as a very important bus driver. He managed to convey his desire to sit next to the driver and 'assist' with the journey, by keeping watch of the traffic and ensuring the driver was going the right way, all of which he was very proud to achieve. I even gave him a special hat to wear for this most important role. The hat magically ensured he had a fixed smile during the whole trip.

While this experience gave him enormous joy, he understood about being caring and sharing with others too. If someone else wanted a turn to assist the bus driver, he would not make a fuss, even though I could see the disappointment on his face. Despite the many emotions I saw him display over the years, his dear older mother, when relating to her 'boy' very lovingly, lamented a sentiment I came across with other people too: "But these people don't have emotions like normal people."

Well, you can imagine how I addressed that comment, albeit sensitively, so she could better understand her lovely 'child'. My comments and examples seemed a revelation to her, and yet she had lived with her son for almost fifty years. I thought long and hard about that attitude of innocent ignorance. I realised how misperceptions may arise and result in considering the disabled as very different from anyone else. Furthermore, I realised how easy it is for the general public to not have the appropriate insights about those who seem different. Even having greater exposure to the disabled does not necessarily ensure we fully understand that we are all, essentially, the same on matters that really count.

Another issue is that some well-meaning people seem to think being disabled means one needs to feel very sorry for them or that they must be liked as individuals, regardless of their personalities. In a sense, I think that both of these views may constitute a form of discrimination. I don't believe that just because a person is disabled means we must like them, as they each have their unique personality, which may or may not be endearing to us. It is no different to any other group within our society. Most of my clients have been pleasurable to work with, but as within any demographic, there may present certain characteristics that I do not necessarily like — it's only natural to prefer certain personality types.

Most importantly in working with the disabled, it is unprofessional and unkind to allow feelings to get in the way of maintaining respect towards each client while providing the best 'duty of care' to each individual. So, if for some reason you feel unable to provide that, then you owe it to them to either find a way that will enable you to work appropriately with them or, if that seems impossible, request a transfer. Negative views about a client or colleague need to be addressed so that all parties function in a positive environment.

As I have suggested, clients can find themselves with an incompatible mix of peers or staff, so it is helpful to be aware when this is the case. All clients in care tend to live with at least four others, and they need to feel as though they don't have to face an antagonistic presence every day. It is their home and they all have the right to feel it is a peaceful and safe environment.

Often clients have no choice about who they share their home with, so it is up to us as carers to be vigilant to each client's emotional comfort level. And this also means the energy you bring to work can either erode or enhance everyone's atmosphere. This cannot be underestimated as a means for generating a sense of group cohesion. No matter the level of your client's disability, or the unique variables of personality types around you, each individual will know how you think and feel about them, based on your manners, tone and unspoken attitude towards them. So always keep in mind that if you show you are willing to give someone a fresh chance, you will be able to make a positive difference to any encounter.

TWELVE

"Every child is a different kind of flower and all together make this world a beautiful garden"
— Unknown

'The looking glass self' is a phrase in psychology that relates to how we may present quite differently in one setting to another. It is the outward expression of behaviours that gives others the sense of our personality 'presenting' type. For example, one mother may see her daughter as a sweet innocent smart thing, who could never do any wrong, yet her close friends or work mates might see her in a completely different light, thus presenting different aspects of her personality (sub-personality) according to whom she is in front of (our mirror). And I have seen this in dramatic ways with my clients, especially those considered the most 'difficult'.

One does need to remember to stand back and consider a given situation from a client's perspective, as many factors feed into how we all behave at different times; even our background experiences can dictate how we interact with certain environmental triggers years later. Indeed, all behaviours relate to a pattern in the brain and this pattern can be altered even with a bit of kindness, understanding and awareness. It might mean thinking differently about any approach to a client.

Over the years, I found that some clients who'd previously lived in a large institution displayed anxious, antagonistic behaviours towards new staff and their peers. After getting to know them, it often seemed to me that their BOC was related directly to their need for self-preservation. In other words, they developed a certain 'persona' which reflected feeling threatened in an open situation where there were many damaged people, including abusive staff. One can only wonder what previous life experiences had driven them to such drastic expressions of behaviour.

With every ID client I ever met, I observed the same eclectic mix of personalities as anywhere; this was evident to the point that if their life circumstances had been different, one could assume their potential of a certain life path. For example, you may recall my 'landscaper' client at the Kevin Heinze garden. Another client named Kerry had the potential to be a great nurturer and loved to look at images of houses, babies and children. This lady yearned to be a mother, and at times she showed sorrow that it would never be. As she tried to say so, her words became blocked and then she'd lose the ability to talk.

I saw many examples over all those years, with clients displaying their personal attributes, all unique and obvious. One who was structured, methodical and most conservative in his manners. Another who loved to follow rock bands, wear bright coloured clothes and comb his hair in strange ways. Some demonstrated their love of painting; others loved nothing more than to garden. I met an avid train collector, and another who loved his footy. The items my clients borrowed from the library were so different — they just seemed to naturally gravitate to certain books too. It was innate.

There are times when I saw the execution of a skill completely disproportionate to the person's apparent level of intelligence. But, then again, one must not forget how one's level of IQ can also relate to having a creative IQ. I personally knew of one lovely lady who could fold washing, including the oddest shaped items, in the most impeccable way — it astounded me. She was an expert at it and took great pride in that task, yet no one ever taught her that skill.

In arts and crafts, I saw those who seemed born with certain skills, such as a middle-aged lady who was able to crochet with unbelievable precision. She only made rugs or doilies, but they were intricately patterned with beautiful scalloped edges. No matter how hard you tried, you could not tell front from back or any start or end point. This perfection was created without any patterns (she couldn't read anyway); it just came from within. This hobby gave her much joy and she loved nothing more than collecting wool of all types and colours.

On this creativity element, I am reminded of an amazing experience during my student years. We had been invited to attend a special lecture to what seemed like a hall full of health professionals. It was a huge privilege as the guest speaker was Elizabeth Kubler-Ross, a world-renowned psychiatrist best known for introducing the 'stages of grief' to the world — something that became a textbook standard, which is still used today.

We were seated in the front row, waiting for the good doctor to appear. I was a little surprised that the lecture was meant to be four hours, with no scheduled breaks. Then this modest-looking person walked onto the stage. She was wearing plain worn-looking, but clean, faded blue jeans and a simple white t-shirt. Short cropped straight brown hair and basic runners completed her image. She didn't need any more adornment as her inner light shone.

The main agenda for Dr Kubler-Ross's presentation that day was about the twenty-plus years she'd spent working with dying children at a special hospice. She had come to recognise how each child expressed their knowledge of the disease stage they were at (mainly cancer) and their knowledge of how long they had before their impending departure. It was through their drawings and paintings that they 'spoke' to her "through their symbolic language" — and they had lots to say about their true feelings:

"I feel sad for mummy."

"I feel the angels are coming soon."

"I am okay."

"I am ready to go."

"It is quite soon. Can I see my brother?"

"I still have several weeks."

"Mum won't let me go."

"I feel scared."

"I need my parents to let me go."

"They came to say they will be with me."

And so on...

These artistic messages helped with follow up counselling for both child and family, helping heal wounds. In particular, it helped many parents let go of their beloved child, knowing how their child needed this, and how their child so often felt at peace about leaving. In many ways, it provided comfort and helped parents overcome their intense grief sooner, especially when their child told them they saw their angel or loved ones around, who told them they would take them by the hand. It was quite usual for the children to paint their angel or deceased loved ones in their artwork, acting as a visual display for how they felt.

Dr Kubler-Ross spoke of how the children were subconsciously conveying their true status. So she used this "symbolic language" to better understand the whole issue of her main theme on death and dying. She also shared a booklet she had made with coloured pens, which was a special letter to a young boy named Dougy, who subsequently passed away. My copy of that booklet, depicting many colourful images and words, is a testament to her spirit.

In the awesome presence of this great lady, we collectively seemed to experience a substantial loss of time that afternoon. She ended her talk after what felt like an hour. But we were all shocked to look at our watches and discover that it had been four hours. To this day, I still don't know how we lost three hours of time, but her inspiration took us to a whole different level.

That experience taught me much about how carers can miss information by only focusing on verbal communication. Much can be conveyed via behaviours or body language. I learnt from Dr Kubler-Ross how we can look to other symbolic processors to get to really know our clients — that special part that resides within the intrinsic self. We can miss the beauty of a person while being too busy forming opinions and judgements of them, especially when we misinterpret their behaviours.

To know how to help bring out the best in anyone is a useful tool, and one that is not always applied to the disabled.

The 'nature/nurture' controversy shows we are all born with certain predispositions, which can be in expression or recession according to our environment. In other words, events and people can bring out the worst or best in us. If you get a chance to find out what motivates your client, then see how much you can do to nurture that 'best' expression. Even with seemingly minor experiences, your clients can surprise you.

I worked in a place that had two ladies who had little or no speech and appeared to light up when taken to see animals at a local farm. These clients were in no way being neglected and had access to soft animal toys and lovely caring staff, but I suspect they simply did not realise how important the connection to the natural world might be. So often that special 'zone within' a person is not that accessible, but it can be revealed in unexpected and special ways. It is a matter of exploring via many and varied experiences. Someone placed in a certain setting may reveal something about themselves quite unexpectedly.

One day I met a client others considered "from hell". She raged obscenities with a raucous voice for no apparent reason, and sounded as if she would hurt someone at any moment. She was described as "a raging bull personality" with an "unpredictable temperament". She threatened to kill herself often and made others feel insecure and frightened around her. No one wanted to work with her and hated it if they did. Such was my introduction to Jane.

Yet my first visit was one of admiration for her beautiful art work — the amazing crocheting I mentioned earlier. She stopped briefly from her concentration to look up as I entered the lounge room where she was seated. I greeted her with a friendly smile. As I walked towards her, I could tell she was working on an intricate complex patterning. Her short brown curly hair framed her deep furrowed brow and ruddy skin, and she looked as though she had a robust body that would kick quite a punch if you got in her way. Yet here was this person weaving the most beautifully delicate piece of work that defied belief. As I neared her, she kept working.

"Oh, what beautiful work, Jane," I said with genuine feeling. "You must be very clever to do that."

"They don't like me here. I hate them all — I hope they die," she uttered with disdain, while working and weaving her beautiful piece.

"Well, I just know you must have some angels on your side to do such lovely work, and look how you are bringing such colour to this place."

I had no idea if she understood me but it just came out. There was no verbal response, but she stopped her work to look at me and she seemed perplexed at what I had said.

"Well, I'm Barbara and I'm pleased to meet you, Jane. I will be coming to work with you soon."

"Can I have a cup of tea?" she asked in a way that seemed more of a test than a question.

"Oh, you like your cuppa too? So do I, and I like a bickie with it, do you? But maybe later?"

Then before she could protest, I added, "In an hour it will be afternoon tea time, so how about I come back then and we can have a cuppa and a chat, okay?" I said, not feeling intimidated by her presence, which I am sure she felt. She knew I had taken control of that conversation and what to expect from me. From the start, I did not focus on Jane's negatives, and believe me they were not imagined — I heard her in full action! But I saw another side to her, which was genuinely lovely.

I found out that Jane had been brought up as a child in a dysfunctional impoverished environment, from which many of her other disabled siblings were taken into care. She also told me how she was abused by her many 'uncles' (a term to be used loosely in this context) and naturally, being of a strong character, rebelled about that in no uncertain manner. It seemed many of the adults in her childhood years could not be trusted to not hurt her. So she used her voice as protest. Over fifty years later, it seemed she was still doing that to staff or to those she didn't trust.

What a pattern to live by, this constant state of vigilance and self-protection. By focusing on her lovely artwork, she saw me as someone who understood her just a little and, over time, she revealed a side of herself I suspect few ever saw. It was sweet, vulnerable, gentle, loving, insightful and authentic. Our relationship became built on trust and honesty. She knew I respected her and I also taught her about my right to be respected. She even started referring to me as her teacher. But when she became annoyed with me for not giving in to a demand, she referred to me as "crabby nurse".

Mind you, she was street wise enough to try her bravado on me, but she knew I knew her too well and her rage amounted to nothing. Once we were at a large hospital in Melbourne and I was escorting her to yet another specialist appointment. This exercise, which was mildly stressful for her, was followed by a trip to the canteen. She loved earning her cuppa and cake treat and was generally very patient and compliant, which I needed her to be in such a busy environment

That day things didn't start very well as our taxi was delayed and Jane became impatient. She asked if we could have our cuppa first. Unfortunately, we had no time and still had to get to a higher floor. She seemed to accept the rationale of my explanation, but was not happy! So, there we were, standing by the lifts with Jane in a rather grumpy mood. And the lift doors did not open. Several loooooong minutes later, the doors still remained shut and Jane became frustrated. By then a large crowd had built up behind us. Doctors, patients, visitors — more and more every second — and still not one lift of three opened their doors. Jane started her tirade. I assured her for the umpteenth time that the lifts would come soon.

"NO, those lifts aren't coming now. You're a liar. Liar!"

"They won't be long," I said in reassuring tone, which she was clearly having none of and I must confess, I was beginning to doubt myself too.

"No, they're not coming. I want to go now. I'm not waiting here anymore!"

The tension was building up behind us; it was so tangible that I felt sorry for the people, who would have been feeling insecure about this 'mad woman' that was starting to sound violent and unpredictable. I almost read their minds wondering if they dared stay or move away. But knowing Jane well, I knew she was huffing and bluffing to get me to take her to the canteen now and with me not complying, she started to get really LOUD.

"IT'S TAKING TOO LONG. THESE BLOODY SHIT LIFTS, THEY WON'T COME NOW. THEY WONT COME — YOU'RE A LIAR. LIAR!"

The tension had built to a critical degree behind us. This was no way to present my client to the wider community in order for her to become more accepted. And worse, that innocent public had no idea of her 'violent' potential. Knowing all that, I hesitate to say that I continued to see the humorous side of the situation. So as Jane paused briefly from her colourful 'street' language to draw breath, I instinctively turned to the crowd behind me and posed the question, "Don't you ever feel like this when the lifts won't come?"

The response was immediate. I felt the tension dissipate as shoulders dropped and — best of all — Jane started to giggle with hands covering her mouth like a little girl. In fact, she giggled all the way to the upper floor — once the lifts arrived soon after her outburst. Many of those brave souls filled our lift, and I imagine they felt proud they had stuck this drama out for as long as they did. After seeing the specialist, Jane had her cuppa and cake. I told her she did a good job as she remained polite, patient and happy — other than that 'blip' in the radar, which she apologised for.

Another time Jane presented a different persona was when I visited her in hospital after she'd fractured her ankle. She greeted me as if she was a loving aunt. She spoke in a sweet voice, so endearing and polite, ensuring I sat in a comfortable chair, thanking me for some items I'd brought her and asking how the others were at her home. Her thoughtful attention towards me was genuine. I wished I had taken a video of her then, as no one could imagine she could be so kind. But I knew she had her way of shielding her true self.

This gruff exterior of hers must have served her well during her difficult childhood and years in the institution. It may well have become her lifeline in certain abusive situations. I especially knew this was how she felt when she asked me who would be on night duty. She liked it when one particular staff member with a 'strong' personality was on because she felt relaxed in knowing she would control the other clients. She always lived in a state of some perceived threat to her wellbeing. That harshly engrained belief system held strong all her life. I could tell that she rarely trusted anyone.

I found this sad to know how the legacy from her past left her fraught with such angst, especially at night when she felt safest in the presence of someone she considered intimidating. She would remain in her room and be able to sleep without anxiety. During the day, she was ever watchful and ready to pounce as her cloak of protection covered her. Mind you, I know she did have an antagonistic element to her nature, but her environment most certainly helped bring it out more; she also tended to manifest that pattern when it suited her. At times, it was merely to get her own way, which evidently worked for her.

Fortunately, Jane had the ability to listen to reason and appreciate that there was another way — although that was something she struggled with. Thankfully, she recognised kindness and respect, even in the face of a firm tone, or a fair and reasonable suggestion — but only if she trusted that person.

Amongst many dramatic incidences, there was one special one I witnessed from Jane: this fearsome lady with a lion's roar, so often causing many innocent staff to flounder and depart the room in tears. One day when she was seriously ill from a long-term condition, I called in to see her; I knew she was dying. Her impeding demise was never mentioned to her but, like Dr Kubler-Ross's dying children, Jane used a metaphor of the clouds to express what she knew was imminent. She was weak and spent most of her time in bed, often having no desire for her beloved cuppa.

As I walked into her room, I saw her looking out the window. Her abandoned craftwork piece, which she'd started forming many months earlier, sat beside her on her 'dressing gown table', as Jane called it. Her wardrobe ('locker' to Jane) was filled with so many colourful pieces, representing the colours of her mind. I knew this because we'd often talked about them. She spoke in a wistful tone. "I can see the angels up there, and I think my mother is up there too in those clouds," she said while appearing very relaxed as the sunlight filled the room, bathing her in a lovely glow. She never expressed anything religions before to me.

"I'm sure you're right, Jane, and one day you'll be able to meet your mother again and share a cuppa while you show her your lovely craftwork — something to look forward to," I offered as I saw her misty smile form.

Standing in silence beside Jane, I wondered what her mother's life had been like as a child and how her life became so difficult, with so many babies taken away from her. Had she watched them from some distant space beyond the clouds after she'd died? What was her pain?

I was then reminded of something I saw during my welfare course. It was a black-and-white photo from the forties of two filthy naked little boys who'd been tied to a bed for several days. I remember feeling such rage when I saw that photo and heard about how their parents often left them alone, too busy drinking and taking drugs. Who were these cruel people who could neglect such little children like that? I couldn't understand and I could barely focus on the horror.

However, just a few pages on, I read about how those boys' parents had been treated as children. I cannot repeat it here. My sense of rage immediately turned to compassion. I had to forgive myself for my hasty condemnation and I will forever feel that no one can ever judge anyone else, as you can't know what their frame of reference for life has been.

So I waited for Jane's response about looking forward to a cuppa with her mum.

"Yes, I'm going to do that," Jane responded, and with her lingering smile, remained in that warm sunlight in an atmosphere of peace and serenity. It was as if pure love encircled her heart.

I stood there for a while, watching and knowing that was the last conversations we would share.

THIRTEEN

"Truer than true... There is no one alive who is you-er than you"
— Dr Seuss

As I look back over the years, I can see why certain individuals stand out in my mind — they were the ones who taught me the most. On that note, this next story recalls how I stumbled on a renewed approach to a long-term dilemma for staff, and one which has potentially serious ongoing health implications for a client. It was all about a little lady called Jodie, who had previously lived in an institution and was well-known for eating cigarette butts. With her small frame and thin hair, it seemed a puff of wind would blow her over. Yet she was a tough cookie, and always keen to know everything that was going on with everyone.

Jodie also engaged in repetitive chatter all day — something staff needed to be able to ignore. It was as if she verbalised every single thought in her head. Some staff were not able to relate to her, and her mistrust and frustrations often tended towards erratic — even violent — behaviour. For that reason, many staff did not want to work with her, and I suspect she knew that. She was easily conflicted but would listen to reason if matters were carefully explained to her and she trusted the one saying it — not an unfamiliar theme. Still, close observation was needed at all times to protect her from harm.

Jodie was also endearing; she had a good sense of humour, was always vigilant of her surroundings and never missed an opportunity — she could be gone and out of sight within seconds. Plus, she was acutely observant of how other's felt and if you were looking a bit serious or silent, she would notice and comment, asking many questions. Once I accidently rubbed hand cream into my eye, which began to water. This resulted in Jodie showing concern. "Are you crying, Barbara? What's wrong? Aren't you feeling well? Aren't you happy?" she asked with genuine interest, and then when we met up days later followed that up with, "Are you feeling better now?"

She had simply dismissed my hand cream explanation as she only responded to my apparent tears. It took time to get to really know her well, and often staff only saw the disruptive behaviours that put her in the 'too hard box'.

Over twenty years earlier, Jodie had been diagnosed with pica, a condition that involves having a compulsion to consume strange or even distasteful items, such as leaves or toxic substances and, as in Jodie's case, cigarette butts from anywhere she could find them. In those days they were everywhere! Even if you saw the butts first, she was quicker and could grab a whole handful from a public container or off the ground and shove them in her mouth before you got there. I made it my challenge to find a solution, but made little progress. Even bribing her with things she loved and rarely had, such as a can of Coke, was of no use. While I managed to minimise Jodie's contact with the butts with acute diligence for her health's sake, it was a struggle.

During that time, her doctor wanted to perform tests on a regular basis to see how matters were internally. The staff at her day program became so concerned they requested we put her on special nicotine patches to address her apparent addiction. It became a contentious issue as I resisted this approach and was backed up by her doctor, who agreed it may do her health more harm than good. I also suspected she was not addicted to nicotine, but merely felt compelled to consume the butts. She also had to be protected from over-consuming water, which can result in a potentially fatal electrolyte imbalance.

In those days, it was difficult to avoid cigarettes, especially with the decree of ensuring our clients integrated into the community. There was even an open ashtray outside the doctors' rooms, which was replaced with a closed unit on my request. When matters were at their worst, I actually stumbled across a solution that even questioned Jodie's pica diagnosis — such is the way something appears out of the blue.

While it was difficult to engage Jodie in anything for very long — besides endless chatter — she did enjoy going on "bush walks" around a nature reserve near her home. It seemed as if the experience drew out something special from within her. She appeared more mature during our walks, showing concern for those walking with us. This experience evidently served to soothe her from certain stressful mental sensations as well. I sensed she was in her 'natural' state on these walks, as she remained completely calm, serene and very cooperative.

I recently saw some scientific evidence for this phenomenon in a documentary. The research related to subjects being linked to wires on their head and a screen that showed the parts of the brain that lit up while viewing selected images. The outcome suggested the beneficial health impacts of merely looking at nature landscapes on a screen as opposed to looking at a more urban scene or streetscape.

At times on our walks, we would pause for a while to sit on a garden bench. I would observe Jodie looking out at the surrounding paddocks; she seemed peaceful and reflective as if she was trying to make sense of her world. This pattern of behaviour was in direct contrast to her more active observation style while indoors. During these outdoor experiences, Jodie gave her voice a rest as she actually stopped her incessant dialogue. Unfortunately, while such 'nature' experiences can be enhancing ones, they require the time and inclination of staff, and I know it is not always possible with staffing requirements. Nevertheless, it is always worth considering any opportunity. But back to the pica experience.

One particular day was rather cold, so we were wearing hats and coats on our walk. All was calm until Jodie spotted a cigarette butt on the side of the path nearby. Too late to do anything about it, she swiftly bent over to scoop it up like an automated robot. But just prior to consuming it, I casually suggested she could place her butt in her coat pocket to "save it for later". To my surprise, she complied and kept walking, seemingly unconcerned about the butt in her pocket. I even offered to give her a plastic bag later, which she evidently thought was a great idea as she reminded me about it when we returned. Perhaps it was the natural environment that opened her to this new way of doing things, but it worked.

I suspect Jodie liked the idea of no longer being placed under pressure to fight for her butts, as she was simply allowed to pick them up and place them in her bag. It ensured she had a constant supply. The result of this event was that I never saw her consume them again. My strategy was that each time I saw her, I offered to give her a clean bag. In order to do this, I would empty most of her cigarette-butt filled bag in the bin and leave a few in the new bag. She watched me do this and never protested that I emptied most, as long as I kept a few for her. She always seemed very satisfied with this arrangement and even proud at how well she managed to collect so many butts. Given the bag was always full, she evidently did not need to consume any of them.

While this offered a reprieve from potential health issues, I tried to switch her collecting to something less 'dirty' — feathers. When we walked, I would pick feathers up while Jodie watched, holding her prized bag of filthy butts. At one time, she asked me ever so sweetly, "Why are you collecting those silly feathers? They look dirty." Clearly switching to collecting feathers was never going to be Jodie's forte.

This experience of finding a solution to Jodie's need to consume cigarette butts alerted me to the value of looking for ideas outside the usual range of investigation. There were no apparent answers that satisfied the staff's need to keep her safe without creating anxiety to all parties. Yet we discovered an agreeable, and infinitely healthier, solution right under our eyes.

On the subject of nature walks, I felt it imperative to encourage every one of my clients to engage in some form of daily exercise, and walking was a much-loved activity that meant getting fresh air and sunshine. Many clients found nature a joyful and calming influence. It helped that their doctor prescribed walking as a daily tonic as it formally justified engaging in this experience, and I decided to have it written up in reports as recommended, whenever possible.

At times I took some wheelchair-bound clients around their residential block. They tended to be ones that did not speak at all and I was pleased to see how they engaged with their eyes, taking in the varied scenes: different-sized homes, gardens, flowers, trees, animals and cars, which all must have appeared so different than their usual view from a vehicle. I would ramble on about this or that but was never sure how much was taken in, as there was no verbal feedback — only occasional focus and smiles.

One time I was approaching a small garden on someone's nature strip with Amy; she was not one to show much emotion but I spoke to her anyway, pointing out things as we passed them. Then I called for her attention to the lovely floral display around a tree. I felt that as it was on the nature strip, I just might pick some for her, stating that "we" were being naughty. I told her she was now my partner in crime and hoped no one was looking out the window. "Now, Amy, you keep a look out and if you see anyone, tell me and we will run. Okay?"

My only consolation was that there were plenty of flowers left. So somewhat sheepishly, I picked a pretty bunch and off we hurried — or tried to, as our getaway was thwarted by a stuck wheel. So we were off down the path, with the posy held tightly in Amy's hand, moving back towards her home. All this activity was without her indicating any focus on what we had just done. But at least she did not let go of the 'stolen goods'. When we entered the house, we met a staff member and explained our devious crime. To my surprise, Amy began giggling like one would if they knew they had done something naughty and were relishing in it. I realised it was her way of telling that other staff member about our 'secret' act, and so we laughed along with her.

It was obvious Amy understood the essence of our deed, and it reminded me to always consider how clients might be thinking or feeling, and to be careful and sensitive to what is being said in front of them. It is so easy to take this thing called respect for granted. I know I have broken this rule many times in simply sharing things with staff or relatives about clients. I realised how this was not appropriate, even if it seemed innocent enough. However, one can include a client in conversation as long as it is something they might like to hear. And my clients always loved hearing gossip!

Another dear lady was also living in that same residence. Lucy was like a sweet little pixie, but she never spoke in the time I knew her, even though she had done so several years previously. So, often I would tell her that I wished she could tell me what she was thinking. I made it a rule to personally greet all the clients by name whenever I arrived, and Lucy always looked directly in my eyes. It was her saying hello in return. While most of the time she was conveyed by wheelchair — and a harness/hoist system was required for her bath — she was able to bear her body weight as long as she was supported upright. Given she was relatively small and light, I would hold her waist from the back to help her walk, which she seemed to enjoy.

Lucy managed this with good strength, but we must have looked awkward and funny. Once one of her soft slippers came off her foot, and I mentioned how we must look like a couple of "drunk bunnies". Well, with that, she laughed and kept it up the whole way. Later on I told her if she liked that joke I could tell her some funny 'rude' jokes, and she laughed even more, especially when I added she could probably tell me a few of her own too — a missed opportunity for 'facilitated communication' perhaps? I felt so regretful that she was unable to share her thoughts.

On another walking expedition, I was taking a couple to the local library. I was a step or two ahead of them when I spotted a beautifully coloured large beetle in the middle of the pathway. Anxious that no one would stand on it, I picked it up and moved it to the grass. I stood aside to wait for the others when I noticed one person saw the beetle and hurried to squash it before I could shout out to stop. Evidently, the intention was to deal with this 'creepy crawly'. I just stood there in utter disbelief.

"Oh no!" I exclaimed in a shocked horrified manner. "I was saving that!"

"Oh, I'm sooo sorry, Barbara," said she, looking between myself and the beetle, worried at how squashed it looked and how upset I looked.

After a slight pause, she came up with a solution. "I-I'll get you another one," was the genuine offer with the notion of me wanting to 'collect' it.

The innocence of it all, thought I, as I reassured her that it was alright, I didn't want another one, but "thank you anyway".

I didn't have the heart to explain what I meant, so no harm done (except to the poor beetle). But I did suggest we don't kill little insects just because they may look a bit creepy, and that they won't hurt us as long as we leave them alone. Thankfully, she seemed to forget about this incident as soon as we entered the library — while I evidently never have!

FOURTEEN

"The minute you feel like giving up,
think of the reason why you held on so long"
— Unknown

One of the most difficult aspects about someone with a disability is them not being able to communicate properly, which can lead to misunderstandings. It means that so much can be missed about that person. Of course, all forms of communication can be employed, but so often in the earlier years of my work this was a haphazard approach, with staff untrained in such matters, and with great variation to each client's ID level. However, at a time when I worked in the Life Education Unit, the Makaton 'symbol' system was being put forward as a viable tool for helping our clients communicate.

While it did offer some insight into what one wanted, the teaching content for the client's emotional information was limited to a standard set of symbols that depicted a range of everyday activities, such as eating, sleeping, or travelling in a car, plus basic universal facial expressions: sad, angry, happy, etc. Photos also offered some insights and photo communication boards or booklets were developed for individuals who required one. Naturally, one's demeanour offered some insight too. Yet there was so much more to know beyond the behaviour set each client was engaged in, but that was mostly how we assessed what was going on for those who had no speech. This proved to be unreliable, as I felt some clients were indicating a certain emotion because that's what they thought was expected of them according to past experiences; their behaviours didn't necessarily match their true feelings or intentions. Sometimes a character trait or pattern of behaviour may emerge only in a specific setting.

One obvious example was with two young adult siblings who had lived in supported accommodation since their mother became unwell many years prior to my meeting them. For years they had spent weekends with their mother on a monthly basis, where they had presented with 'negative' behaviours in terms of verbal and physical abuse towards her. After the mother passed away, a relative took over caring for them one weekend a month as a promise to the sibling's mother.

Unfortunately, this lady was severely burdened by that fact that each time they were visiting for the weekend, the pair continued to present that abusive behaviour they had towards their mother. I can only imagine how that poor mother had coped with that. Perhaps she thought that because her children were so disabled they couldn't help it. It would be so easy to cave into threats for this or that and easy to see how such a pattern can be learned. Likewise, this relative who took on the mother's role also believed that because of their disability, they could not help their behaviour.

I have known how some family members, as loving as they are, seem convinced their disabled relative cannot learn beyond what they are presenting due to their 'condition'. Anyone is able to manipulate their environment in order to achieve a desired outcome but it is up to us to teach all children, regardless of any disability, the most appropriate way to do so. I have seen how some of the smartest or sweetest children try to manipulate their family as a means to achieving a goal, only to find there is another way, and one that has positive outcomes for all concerned. Often it just means they need to learn how to do so in the most appropriate way.

When I heard about this woman's burden, I welcomed the chance to speak with her as I knew this destructive pattern must end. Sure I felt concerned for her, but I also felt that allowing it to go on was inadvertently doing those two siblings a disservice. I even privately wondered if the violent pattern had begun by the siblings watching someone else abuse their mother. Not wishing to intrude into the past potential family dynamics, I focussed on the situation at hand. Had things continued like that, the stress building up would have meant future home visits would not have been possible, which would have been a shame with all family members missing out on some positive and loving contact.

"So, I can tell that you are very reluctant to have them at your home now and even a little scared?" I asked the lady, who was wrenching her hands and looking anxious.

"Well, I just don't know what to do. It was a promise, you know, and I would hate to go against that. I would have to carry that guilt of breaking a promise to their mother. But recently we have had to call the police for something and I can't seem to do anything to put an end to this awful situation — it is getting worse."

"How do you find them generally — I mean when they are not doing that nasty behaviour?"

"Well, they seem quite pleasant really and we can have fun too. It's just that they then seem to spoil it, and one seems to copy the other one."

"And do you suggest any consequences or offer any warnings or explanations?"

"What do you mean? I can't punish them."

"No, of course not, but if they continue to do as they are, everyone is unhappy and I suspect those two have learned this behaviour and, in a way, are doing what they think is expected of them. That is a possibility. I would suggest also that, most likely, they hate being that way and reprimanded too. So what do you say to them about their behaviour?"

"I tell them that if they continue like they are, they may miss out on all the things they like doing, or that they might not be able to come again."

"Have you ever followed up on that?"

"Well, no. I would just feel too guilty in doing that. My words just remain a threat, that's all."

"May I make a suggestion as I can see that this is only going to escalate and you already seem to be at your limit of stress. Am I reading that right?"

"Yes, I do need some advice as I get stressed all month now, just anticipating them coming, and they have become more abusive and I am feeling a bit scared too."

"Okay, my first suggestion is to actually agree to establish some clear and definite consequences, which you must follow through on. My suggestion is to return them the very moment they start their nasty behaviour. I don't mean several warnings and then you act — you must take action at the very first 'offence'. If you don't follow up, then they will perceive you as weak and will feel in control. They may not even want that, as strange as that may seem. But first you must ensure you state clearly what you will do and why, and ask them if they understand, can you do that?"

"I don't know."

"Then you are going to have to be brave and believe you are doing it for their benefit. It can't be fun always being in trouble, and I feel sure that they want to enjoy happy relationships with their family. You feeling anxious around them would impact on their energy too, as that's how it works with us all. I can see that you hold the cards with this, and they need you to display strength, just like rebellious teens need to have reasonable boundaries."

I did not give her time to protest so I continued. "Many people think that just because someone has an ID, they are unable to learn or understand how to manage themselves more appropriately. They are not given credit for what they can do or want to do. So we make too many allowances that harm, then with unwanted behaviour, they become disliked and thought of negatively. That is a disservice to them and to everyone involved. The basics of psychological conditioning works the same for us all, disabled or not."

"I never thought of it that way... I suppose I could try a different approach."

"Well, I honestly think you can do it but give me a call if you need some emotional reinforcements, and please remember that unless you do change this situation, it may be that you become too stressed or unwell and then not available to keep your promise. Remember, you are important too and you deserve respect. You can lovingly provide those two with structure, then they have a chance to feel good around you."

So the next scheduled month's visit arrived and the excited siblings were travelling along when they had the proposed 'consequences' explained to them. All understood but as soon as they arrived at their destination, one sibling started the 'nasty' behaviour and, to my delight, I was told that it resulted in an immediate return. However, the other one, who did not misbehave, remained.

I found out that once the instigator was returned to their residential facility, there were no presenting negative behaviours by them for the remainder of the weekend. Then on the following and all subsequent visits, both siblings were well behaved and looked forward to future visits. That long-term problem disappeared, and words of warning turned to words of praise.

I once worked around another young man in his early twenties, Rodney, who looked like a cute-faced three year-old — except for the fact that he was nearly seven feet tall. Seeing a three year old throw a tantrum because they didn't get what they want is interesting enough, but seeing a grown man, and a very tall one at that, react in a similar way becomes scary and violent. So this young man was in need of a 1:1 staffing schedule 24/7. I suspected his 'tantrums' were merely learned behaviour and that perhaps his loving family allowed him to have what he wanted when he acted this way. Nevertheless, it was determined he could learn to manage a more appropriate strategy in order to satisfy his needs or wants. Slowly, over much time, he was shown how to deal with achieving goals in an appropriate manner.

Naturally, as with any tantrum presentation, it required

much patience and consistency from staff. The issue of consistency cannot be overstated. For a client, the fear of not knowing what to expect, often exacerbated by a high turnover of staff, can be the single most relevant cause of unwanted behaviour. Sure, plans of management are written up in order to maintain a uniform approach, but the different personalities of staff can result in a different interpretation, or even application, of the plan.

To ensure staff are not likely to be absent due to stress is often up to the quality of management of any facility. Ensuring staff feel supported and valued is an important key to maintaining a harmonious environment for all concerned. 'To value front line staff is to value clients' makes a worthy mantra, but it is not often well executed.

Much can be hidden when a client is either unable or unwilling to explain why they do as they do. Looking for insights provides opportunities that would otherwise be missed.

One dramatic case from over twenty-five years ago helps illustrate this point; the events are still vivid in my memory. I was on a casual shift in a facility in Canberra where a young man in his twenties lived. Micky had Down syndrome and rarely spoke but seemed otherwise smart. He had moved from interstate to a new abode and appeared happy and settled there, as well as seemingly adjusted to his day programs. But one day he simply disappeared.

Micky's normal routine was to leave at a certain time of the morning, travel on a bus to the day facility, and at the end of his day retrace his steps, without incident. However, that day at around 4pm, the staff at his home wondered why he hadn't returned. The day program staff reported he hadn't arrived that morning and they'd concluded his home staff must've forgotten to phone — something that should always be followed up on.

I had arrived for evening duty when informed of this and by then the police were involved. By 9pm there was still no sign or clue of his whereabouts. The frantic staff had covered all possible leads. At around 10pm I received a phone call.

"Hello, I am the station master of Spencer Street Station in Melbourne. I have a young man here by the name of Micky, and this number was in his wallet. Do you know him?"

"Sorry? Are you joking? This is Canberra you know?" I blurted in my least professional manner. "Do you really mean he is actually there in Melbourne?"

"Well, yes, but he is not saying much other than his name and one more word that sounds like 'uncle'. Was he supposed to visit him in Melbourne? We have no address, but for now he doesn't appear agitated or upset — he's quite relaxed."

After I explained where he left from that morning, there was stunned silence before we exchanged details, ensuring the intrepid traveller was cared for overnight until he could be returned the next day. It was straight forward, and the station master was wonderfully helpful and understanding.

I didn't know Micky well enough at that time, but it was a remarkable thing for him to depart at 8am in Canberra and arrive at 10pm in Melbourne. It meant he took his normal bus to a different depot in the city, rather than to his much closer day program location. Then he would have had to take a bus to a station on the outskirts of Canberra to catch a train to another station. This was a daily coordinated bus/rail link with the NSW Trainlink and Vline. As he did not have funds, I couldn't even imagine how he had worked that all out, managed his day (Toilet? Food?) and successfully arrived in Melbourne. No one believed he was capable of that achievement — talk about underestimating our clients!

It turned out a visit to some uncle was not viable and was explained to Micky when he arrived back in Canberra via a plane ride. There appeared to be no negative outcome for the 'happy wanderer' and, I daresay, he enjoyed the journey. It was impossible to know how long he had planned that or if it was a spontaneous decision. Likewise, we did not know if he had been missing his uncle, as he was unable to express his feelings to anyone. All reports gave no clues, as none of his previous behaviour indicated he was in any way unhappy or unsettled. Indeed, days and weeks after this event, he was seemingly unperturbed by his adventure, or that he never got to meet his uncle. However, I think he was enjoying the attention as it was all a buzz for some time.

It remained a question to me that perhaps someone was remiss in not telling him that his uncle had passed away a few months prior to him arriving at this new facility in Canberra. Thinking we need to protect someone from the potential grief of loss is not necessarily appropriate and certainly not our decision. Grief is a normal part of life and I believe it far more respectful to share and be there for support. To conclude that a disabled person is to be protected is somewhat discriminatory. Everyone has the right to know when a family member dies.

This experience reinforced my belief that we simply cannot know what any disabled person is thinking or feeling about their life, and even our perceptions may not match their reality of what their world looks like. Of course, that goes with almost anyone — even with our loved ones. With most of my interactions, I automatically consider how I might feel should I be in my client's shoes at that given time, under that specific circumstance.

One example of this is how I enter a room when my disabled clients are present; this simple act of walking into a room can generate a positive or negative atmosphere, based just on the way you greet them. Your words, tone and attitude set the emotional tone for everyone. Imagine waking early one morning feeling unwell, cold or hungry and wanting to have something warm to drink. The staff aren't ready to make drinks so they yell at you to return to bed.

Another scenario is that you are unable to speak or move much in your bed — you may even be feeling uncomfortable. Suppose you are woken without any warning as someone walks into your bedroom and switches the main light on, flooding your eyes with brightness and — with no time to adjust — gives you your medication. I promise you, like myself, you would hate it and resent it but that does happen.

This is not to say the staff who might do that are not caring people, but may be preoccupied or overloaded with tasks and just don't think. Sometimes it may take a bit of awareness to realise how our own behaviour can impact others. I know this can happen in nursing homes also, when the staff have limited time to shower too many residents, far too early in the morning, as they have a tight agenda. I understand that available funds often dictate how many staff need to cover a set number of tasks over a given time. Such staff can feel the pressure and guilt of such time restrictions.

It may help to realise, however, at a certain age, conditions of the disabled and elderly can become blurred — we all will be older some day!

FIFTEEN

"Being disabled should not mean being disqualified from having access to every aspect of life"
— **Emma Thompson**

I want to relate how we are dealing with our disabled these days, well away from the trenches of ignorance, cruelty and discrimination, towards a bright new image of the disabled in our land... Um, did I just say that?

The World Health Organisation (WHO), in their October 2013 World Health Report, claimed one in four people around the world will be affected by mental or neurological disorders at some time in their life. Naturally, this view encompasses a whole range of disabilities. But narrowing it down to Australia and — more specifically — ID, the 2009 Australian Bureau of Statistics Survey of Disability, Agencies and Carers showed that there are well over half a million people with an ID and the number is ever growing (the outcome of this survey was used to inform the Victorian State Disability plan 2013-2016). This translates to a huge ongoing need for ruling governments to understand what processes work best in the interest of the intellectually disabled and their families.

To the question "Are we there yet?" I can confidently say

we have made fantastic strides forward in how we care for and encourage ID individuals towards improved living conditions, enhanced opportunities and better standards for carers to follow. The pendulum of change began swinging wildly during the 1980s with the closure of the large institutions. Typically, when staff are confronted with change, especially if there seems to be relative harmony in the camp amongst staff, there is trepidation and resistance to those changes. However, when the changes eventually are implemented, it is often perfectly acceptable and even beneficial.

Psychologically there is a tendency to fear the unknown, and it would help reduce stress if all staff are informed about what the impending changes entail and how they can help formulate them. Often paperwork precedes a change — even years prior — without much explanation, and that can generate all kinds of gossip based on conjecture and misinformation. Unfortunately, the experience so often becomes a case of 'them and us'.

One such example happened during the eighties. It was decreed that ID clients would be supported in gaining jobs with external employers, along with significant reduction of their recreational pursuits. If the clients engaged in those, they required formal justification in written form, followed by detailed documentation — if they were allowed at all. In fact, the many recreational pursuits were not given much credence as being relevant to the client's overall development. Naturally, there were protests from the front line staff, who were never questioned about this new 'innovation' of jobs.

I recall how one facility with over eighty clients had to consider all of them for supported employment. Yet the reality was that only three were vaguely suitable for unsupervised work.

When the 'trialled' clients went through the obligatory hands-on support (which was eased off gradually and phased out after six months), those clients returned to their day placement, as the pressure was too great for them. From a simple conversation with one eager young man, I could tell he felt as though he had failed when previously he'd felt proud about his abilities with a gardening group 'business' that the facility operated.

It proved the policymakers, who most certainly meant well, were somewhat misguided; in their haste for change they were not willing to listen to reason when initially informed that employment was not an option for most of the ID clients there. It was not about the staff being negative, but after spending years of direct contact with their clients, they knew what motivated them best, and what gave them pride and joy — and even what their general capabilities were. Eventually, for that group of clients at least, the more recreational rather than vocational pursuits returned, but with more structure and planning. This was a good thing. So as can happen with anything drastically new, the pendulum swung back to sensible levels with a positive overall outcome.

When these hard-working policymakers realised they got that employment issue wrong, they supported a new approach by starting a process that provided all clients with a formal opportunity to say what they wanted, needed and enjoyed most. For those without speech, their behaviours provided meaningful information to staff, but also, a variety of supported communication formats, such as sign language, image boards and photos were used towards helping each individual make a decision. This saw the creation of IPPs (related in chapter two), which required full documentation regarding objectives, activities and outcomes within a specified time in order to have the plans implemented. The new emphasis on care became based on the 'individual's potential'.

Along with that new focus came much emphasis on staff meetings, training, documentation for intentions and outcomes, etc, all of which meant paperwork overload took on a life of its own. However, this new format served its purpose during the transition from a 'custodian care' approach to one focused on respect towards each individual, guided by a worthy set of standards. The focus was designed to help move an individual towards what they wanted, needed and were capable of. It forced staff to consider new ideas and possibilities for each client. But the flip side was it generated critics from staff who felt their clients were pushed into new programs too quickly in order to satisfy policy agendas. This was a contentious issue.

Nevertheless, it all helped the disabled being perceived as worthy citizens in their own right. Now that those IPPs have morphed into Person Centred Plans (PCP) still with primary emphasis on the individual as it places more focus on what the client needs or prefers than what policy dictates they might need or desire — the emphasis is on personal choice. I generally don't criticise this ongoing process as policymakers had to learn on the run, so to speak, while they were under pressure from human rights groups to ensure justice was being done for the disabled. Many lobby groups feared that once the institutions closed, many residents would be left abandoned and neglected. The ruling government worked hard to prevent that.

The introduction of the National Disability Insurance Scheme (NDIS) has ensured worthy opportunities for the disabled, and is designed to deliver maximum support and benefit required for each disabled individual and their family. Needless to say, this NDIS must be cost effective and relevant to a wide range of needs. While in principle this new scheme sounds positive, only time will tell how it goes in practice. From its implementation on 1 July 2016, I wonder how many modifications there will be to the scheme to improve it.

There are already detractors who claim that some people who have been receiving a disability pension for genuine reasons may find themselves on the outer. While it needs to be tested over time, I remain hopeful that more positives will result than negatives, and feel it will serve as another learning curve for how our society treats its disabled overall.

Above all, this activity of change sits under the guidance of the Universal Declaration of Human Rights (1948), and the Charter of Human Rights and Responsibility Act 2006 (CHRR), which was reviewed in 2015 with over twenty recommendations. It is a law with a wide set of complex legalities, around twenty basic principles, related to equality and freedom. In essence, it promotes the values of equality, respect, dignity and worth of all citizens.

For the staff who worked with the ID during the time of this renewed emphasis on justice for all, we had access to posters that promoted the ideals of care for the disabled, which included a summary of 'The Charter' as a large colourful page of the CHRR. The new 'person centred' approach promoting 'choice' is considered a critical issue under NDIS. The terminology embedded under the banner of the Charter is a good indication of how far we have come from those early changes made in the late eighties. But as with everything that sounds ideal, the proof of how well those ideals get translated into reality is to observe and assess what happens at ground level for each individual client and their family. Only then can we measure the true quality of their life.

It is noteworthy how the main springboard for growth from that old style of care was the 1985 'Handicapped Persons Review', as it led to the Disability Services Act of 1986, which provided standards for the provision of goods, services and facilities. It really did reshape the way disability services were funded, as the state took responsibility for the administration of family support, recreation, community access, accommodation and alternatives to employment. It also stimulated growth in vacation care, family respite and holiday camps. Today, it is mandatory to ensure every client living in supported accommodation has one fully supervised holiday each year.

A program known as Community Visitors, made up of dedicated volunteers, agree to visit each residential home. They have the authority to scrutinise client reports and to ensure client's needs are being met and that their homes are appropriated for their unique needs. They even ask clients how they feel things are going, and if some deficit is noted, the visitors can write a formal request to have certain requirements addressed and re-check these things upon subsequent visits.

This revolutionary approach has tried to actively prevent abuse, neglect and violence by working with all networks to provide meaningful participation and active inclusion of the disabled in the whole of society. The hope was that potential bullies could no longer hide behind their vulnerable clients for their own personal expression of power. But the new systems are not completely successful as abuse has occurred, with questionable individuals slipping through the employment net and being placed in responsible positions where they can take advantage of their clients. Hence the emphasis these days for well-scrutinised staff credentials.

During the eighties, much formal training was rolled out for workers in the ID field. I used to constantly hear in meetings the high expectations that we would soon see true 'integration', but I had my doubts due to the lingering general public ignorance towards disability. However, I did see the imperative of our disabled citizens being enabled to have access to a wide range of public facilities. I agreed that the key would be greater exposure of the broad range of disabled people to the wider community in order to slowly promote greater acceptance by the public. I knew from the types of questions people in my personal life were asking that there were still many misunderstandings about what being disabled entails. One such example was when someone asked me when my clients' status of being a 'patient' changed to a client.

That lingering disease-medical model concept of being disabled was still prevalent and my answer was that having a low IQ did not render that person as having a disease. I related that they had not developed beyond a certain intellectual or cognitive level, and that mostly they were healthy individuals who needed our support and guidance, but still had a great capacity to learn and manage their life to their fullest potential.

Another question related to how dangerous they were to work around, as if they were going to spring to some violent attack without provocation. I replied that any of us could potentially succumb to some form of mental illness, if left untreated, and also might be prone to some aberrant behaviour, given the right circumstances. This connotation of an ID person being sick and dangerous sprang from intelligent and reasonably minded people. They were in no way stupid or uncaring, but merely ignorant of the facts. Nevertheless, this was the time when 'integration' was the new buzzword for ID.

At the time, I debated and argued that it would be a two-step process, starting with 'co-existence' long before true 'integration'. I felt that if more disabled people mingled amongst the general population, it would help reduce ignorance, misunderstanding and fear. I appreciated that the policymakers were indeed going to achieve that first step. After all, it was not that long ago people were locked away from view, as if they were somehow negative elements within society to be kept separate. So a resounding "yes" to exposure and opportunity, but even now, thirty years later, I would say that, at best, we have only achieved a reasonable measure of 'co-existence'. True integration will only happen when the general public's attitude towards the disabled significantly improves. But progress is here and I am the eternal optimist!

The advent of day programs is what keeps our ID clients connected to the wider community in many ways. This workable concept was already in play twenty-five years ago within the mushrooming day training centres. These days the system has been taken up by numerous not-for-profit groups, with hundreds of organisations currently registered with the government to provide disability support services, including smaller community service organisations that cater for ID adults who are unable to be employed. Along with the staff who work in the supported accommodation field, these facilities provide employment for people of all ages who want to be involved with the disabled.

The current emphasis is on the overall wellbeing of clients, with the trend being to personally design activities for each individual. These include everything from specific independent living skills training, to community inclusions of all kinds, as well as in-house activities that ensure participants have access to stimulating and joyful experiences. The greater the opportunities, the more each client will be able to make informed choices. From the outline of policies, it is up to the staff to explore and implement the appropriate avenues for each individual. My personal take is that a degree of flexibility is always required to cater for individual differences amongst the clients, as common sense can be neglected if programs are not specifically individualised.

I only say this from experience, and one example is the well-intentioned directive of providing and supporting late afternoon or evening activities for clients, including discos, basketball, outings or dinners as extra community inclusion options. These schedules are welcomed and maximise the client's life experience. Yet while some do enjoy this, and keenly look forward to such events, many are tired after returning from their day programs and prefer to have dinner early and relax for the rest of the evening. Perhaps they prefer to retire to their rooms for some much needed 'time out' from large groups. Any ruling that specifies a time for putting on night wear, having dinner and even retreating to one's room is nothing more than institutional and I have refused to conform to such schedules when it clearly compromised my client's wellbeing.

Rules that don't serve the client appropriately, or are even stressful, are wrong! That issue of flexibility cannot be underestimated. I shall offer you an example. One lady I knew became extremely anxious if waiting beyond 5pm-ish for her dinner, with her upset state ruining her evening. She was not deliberately being demanding, but she became over anxious, unable to control her impulses. Yet with an early meal she relaxed and settled happily, followed by a good sleep. So call me a rebel but even against internal policy I never compromised where the wellbeing of my client was concerned.

I explained why this move was justified and provided documentation to back up my claims. In this instance, certain management staff were not impressed with my attitude. But at a meeting that took place later, a visiting psychologist from Canada stated that such flexibility for each client was appropriate and at times even necessary.

Of course, I do have respect for the worthy standards put in place for both client and staff that specifically set out the 'duty of care' for each individual. Clearly this is important on all levels as, without them, standards can lapse and clients may suffer. But common sense must also prevail and the best outcomes occur when egos don't get in the way. Policy always needs to translate to reality in order to embrace the individual needs of each client. Likewise, there is a strong case for consistency of staffing, as mentioned earlier, as it can take time to build trust, so staff need to be heard at all times. I cannot overstress the imperative of enabling frontline staff to be involved in decisions for their clients. While they are not formally their 'advocates', they must always advocate on behalf of their client, when a need is noted.

Never give up on your client, and look to the process in place that addresses any grievances if your verbal approach is ignored or dismissed. Standing up for your client is an important part of the job. Otherwise, you may as well just be a robot.

SIXTEEN

"People with a disability have abilities too... making sure these abilities blossom and shine so that their dreams can come true"
— Mary Mcaleese

When considering variations to the norm in daily practice, it does pay to understand that because the field of ID deals with people, not systems, we must be open to alternative approaches in different situations. Of course, one must always respect policy and engage in support from management if endeavouring to alter rules. It is a matter of remaining within certain boundaries. Yet as I have shown in previous chapters, one might see something that others have missed, despite well-meaning approaches from previous staff. As disability is a human services field, this aspect of insight and instinct plays a part in the overall development and deployment of support for clients. I have used this approach for the whole of my career and found it greatly beneficial in how I proceed when I observe something needing to be remedied.

Several years ago, a vacant room was to be filled by a new lady, Sally, who, by the time she arrived, was suffering from a serious health condition with a shortened life expectancy.

Prior to her arrival, she had been fiercely determined to live independently and was reasonably able to do so, with programmed support. Her caseworker was given permission to only call in to check on her finances each fortnight. Such was her strong need to fully function without help — she lived alone in a small unit, caught public transport to her place of employment (a nearby factory), organised her own food and did her own domestic work.

Unfortunately, Sally's determination meant she insisted she ate the food she liked, mostly fast food and not appropriate for her health. However, one day, she stopped going to work, and by the time her support workers found out, they discovered her in a dire state alone in bed. After several weeks in hospital, she was placed in a supported residential facility.

Sally's story held mixed emotions for me as I was glad she was able to live more or less independently, as she had wanted. However, with her ID, she lacked the insight over her health status and this lead to her unchecked health decline. She was severely asthmatic, amongst other conditions. A combination of living alone, being too unwell to seek help, and being reported as missing from work only after a week, meant she had been placed in a precarious position. It was deemed she needed to live in supported accommodation.

As one might imagine, Sally was not happy that she wouldn't be returning to her home. I could tell she never fully accepted the need to be placed in the supported accommodation and even resented it. However, as her condition was expected to worsen, the decision to live independently was taken out of her hands. Although she tried to keep a brave face, remaining polite and friendly, it seemed apparent her will to live was gone and she died just a few months later.

I share Sally's story because I have found that those who are acutely aware of their disability status are the ones who fly the highest in feeling they can overcome all odds or dive deepest in the depths of despair when they lose control. Over more than thirty years, I did come across those who were borderline with their ID and being slightly along the IQ line, they were acutely aware of their shortcomings, especially the areas they felt they would not experience. Such 'normal' life opportunities (driving a car, being married, being a parent or holding a job) tended to be out of their radar, and they felt their lack personally and deeply.

For the majority of my ID clients, their approach to life was that they were happy to be respected, their uniqueness appreciated and their days filled with relative comfort, kindness and positive experiences. As long as these aspects were in place, they did not seem to sense overall awareness of any lack. They instead focussed on their positive life experiences. But for the small handful, they felt this lack acutely and carried a deep sense of loss.

From my experience with those borderline ID individuals, it was the level of awareness of their lack that caused more emotional harm than any other issue, and I realised how the greater we focus on our lack, the more difficult life can be. This concept is no different to any of us, but we may be able to consider our lot in a more insightful way. Over the years, I watched most of my clients seem oblivious to much of the angst my colleagues seemed to deal with over their busy lives. A mother of one of my clients once told me that she had two 'normal' children who gave her much trouble and stress over many years, but from her disabled daughter, there was nothing but joy as she always seemed happy and worry-free.

On this topic, I well remember hearing a story that happened in America over twenty-five years ago. A community decided to integrate their ID teens with a group of non-ID teens within a social/friendship setting. I suspect the teens may have only been borderline ID, as they wanted to do this not really knowing what it was going to be like. After a few weeks of this weekly social activity, the ID teens asked to not do it anymore and, from what the organisers could glean from this experiment, the ID group felt their differences much more in the presence of the friendly but 'normal' teens who discussed their cars, girlfriends and prospective careers. I was told they reverted back to their usual social group and events and were happier.

I found this touching that the ID group felt sad they would never engage in such things and did not want to be in a situation that made them feel so different. Such feelings had not been considered by the well-intentioned organisers and I can only assume the ID individuals were acutely aware of their lack and this event had enhanced their personal view. As I said previously, I have only met a small handful of clients with acute awareness of their status, out of hundreds.

That is why anyone working with the disabled must be sensitive to their clients' thoughts and feelings. Still, I don't wish to have someone feel intimidated in an environment they may not feel emotionally comfortable with, but I also would not wish to limit possible opportunities. Alas, with the best intentions, staff don't always get it right.

I will never forget a movie I saw quite by accident many years ago. I remember it was in black and white, so presumably an older movie. What caught my attention was the large building displaying a Mental Health Hospital sign. I was so taken by the storyline that I wrote many details down: title of the movie, the real name of the main character, the location and relevant details as outlined in a passage at the end. I did this as it stated at the beginning that it was a true story written by a friend of the person it was based on.

I fully intended to follow it up for research after my studies. Unfortunately, after moving house several times, all the details were lost. But I will never forget how it influenced me to look beyond what is before me and to not form beliefs, unless I see or experience things for myself. I think it's an important lesson for us all to take everyone on face value, rather than forming preconceived determinations based on other people's perceptions.

I have since tried to look the movie up on the internet, without success. But what I can say is that I was astounded by the way it demonstrated just how much we are influenced by our environment. It is not only about how we may think of ourselves negatively, but to the extent that our whole physical self can present as something it never was. So I shall relate this story as I remember it. At least I will get the essence of the message correct, even if some details are mistaken. I shall call the character in the story Thomas.

The movie was set when institutions were known as 'mental health hospitals' (having moved on from the more archaic 'asylum' heading). The back story was that a certain psychiatrist operated a home for the disabled, which was similar to a small private institution. Years previously, one of his friends had a severely disabled baby. He offered to take care of him from birth and I can only imagine how much the mother had loved that baby but was too devastated to be able to cope with him. She trusted her doctor friend to take good care of her disabled child. She turned her love into a bank account for her son and records indicated she placed funds in it on his birthdays. I presume the mother eventually passed away as there was no mention of her later. Years went by and finally the doctor became ill and passed away too, so that meant the disabled 'inmates' of his small residential care home needed to be rehoused.

A large hospital was designated for their inclusion and the movie began with the day the remaining adults from that residence arrived there — all marching in with limps and disfigured bodies. It made for a sad picture. One of the young men shuffled along with a blanket over his hunched body, and a nurse who was helping with the new intake noticed something about him that caught her attention. She couldn't explain quite what, but she related a certain 'look' he gave that suggested he may not be as cognitively disabled as the others. She asked for permission to work with him on a one-on-one basis but this was refused. Her curiosity was sparked and she persisted, eventually being given permission to do so but only in her own time. So keen was she that she took on this task over many months after each shift.

The amazing outcome of this attention was that from his strangeness of looks, sound and movement, this man's body began to unravel, just as a crushed flower might unfold its petals and open up to a lovely bloom. With no limp, walking upright, he also began to speak. Mind you, her close attention meant she had to teach him to do all these things properly but once shown, he was able to do so well. Overall, it was found he was quite intelligent and so the learning tools became more sophisticated as he gradually demonstrated his natural abilities and full potential. So much so that Thomas requested to leave the hospital and discussions of him moving out and living independently began. In any event, the nurse and a team of three others, who also saw Thomas's potential, agreed to help him.

From the bank account his mother had set up for him, he was able to purchase a small unit and was given a pension for accommodation and living costs. Once everything was set up, he moved out and began a new life. He was visited regularly by his 'team'. The problem was they had become very protective of him and fussed over him with each visit. As much as he appreciated their support, he felt stifled by that ongoing attention and it kept him from feeling 'normal'.

So one day, when his team came to visit, he was not there. He'd just disappeared, but from memory, I think there was a note left expressing his feelings and need to keep separate from them — but that part may not be accurate. Although they were upset and concerned, they respected his wishes to not be found. The final words at the end of the movie stated that no one ever heard from him again. Apparently, his need to cut off all ties from his 'old identity' was so strong. I felt disappointed as I had hoped there may have been some contact, even years later to say that at least he was alright and happily living his life, but not so.

That movie left a great impression on me during my psychology studies, where I learned how that young man likely used the role models within his environment to express himself physically and emotionally. We learnt of cases where 'feral' children had lived for years in the wild. Initially, they made animal sounds for speech and copied their movement too, having learnt these behaviours from the animals — their role models in their environment. In Thomas's case, his role models were predominantly physically deformed, and grunting was often their way of speech, so he picked up on these behaviours.

I spoke to someone who had worked in an institution years earlier and she spoke of a disabled teen who was considered ID. The teen had been locked in the chicken shed and fed scraps as a small child prior to being found and sent into care. The teen would walk stooped over, moving around like a chicken, looking for food. She never really recovered and it may well have been that her brain was not able to — a horrific isolated case.

So with that young man depicted in the movie, he may not have had a low IQ or even been ID — he merely learned his behaviour. When confronted with new possibilities, however, he unwound his distorted view of himself and found out what he was truly capable of. I wonder how many other cases have been similar or worse than his. It seemed somewhat surprising that as an adult he was able to develop his brain, which had 'stunted' at some point during his younger years.

With the advent of the new understanding from 'brain plasticity' research over the past few years, headed by the research psychiatrist Norman Doidge (*The Brain that Changes Itself*), we understand how our brains are capable of learning throughout our entire lives. This provides greater credence to ensure all ID-diagnosed clients are given a chance to develop to their fullest potential — whatever that level may be. I have found that even if their skill level does not advance, the emotional enhancement towards personal satisfaction alone is a worthy goal.

But the point of sharing that previous story is based on

the important theme flowing through my own story here. I have related in several ways that having a positive view of a given situation or person provides the potential to generate a desired outcome. We tend to bring with our interactions — even at a subconscious level — a type of expectation that is reflected in our emotions, terminology, tone and overall behaviour. We may well present this way without being aware of it. So if fear is a dominant belief for a specific situation or person, the outcome may achieve a corresponding negative outcome. From this we can say that, psychologically speaking, by our reaction to anything or anyone, we can create a self-fulfilling prophecy.

Seventeen

"Before you start to judge me, step into my shoes and walk the life I'm living and if you get as far as I am, just maybe you will see how strong I really am"
— Unknown

I have suggested how it is important to be aware of the primary emotions and perceptions that drive us in any given situation — especially if there is some negative element because our prejudices and fears can influence outcomes. An important opportunity for me to apply such a notion was presented when I was introduced to Gina.

I had been informed this lady was being assigned to my area and that she was a person formally under the care of Mental Health. This was quite different to many of my clients who were first given an ID diagnosis, with some later developing a mental illness rendering them in need of psychiatric medication to control their condition. I was told the lady had a psychiatric background, was living in a special house alone with two staff on a 24/7 rotational basis, had acute psychosis and required, along with her huge doses of daily medication, a weekly anti-psychotic injection.

In addition to this, I was informed Gina often required

PRN medication (an additional emergency medication assist) if necessary, and that this was a daily occurrence. However, the ruling was that if/when a second dose of PRN was required, I had to seek permission from the Mental Health section, which was located elsewhere. I immediately thought the management of this arrangement, regarding access and timing, was potentially problematic.

As I am not a psychiatric nurse, I wondered if this new client was being placed suitably, given she had been in and out of psychiatric wards since she was a teenager. But as always, I tried to keep an open mind and awaited Gina's visit where she would be seeing her new home and meeting her female co-residents. I was told she liked reading magazines and enjoyed treats with tea and coffee, so I arranged for the visit to coincide with afternoon tea. As I expected, she duly arrived with two caretakers close by.

For her move a week later, it was deemed necessary for them to remain on-site with Gina over the first twelve days to support her transition. Upon hearing this, I was not sure if that arrangement was workable either, but decided to 'wait and see'. I felt that like all my previous first contacts, it was up to me to set the tone for someone new to feel comfortable in the presence of different surroundings and new faces. So the scene was set.

"Hello and welcome, Gina. I'm Barbara, pleased to meet you," I said as I beckoned her through the door. "I'll be working with you soon. I am looking forward to getting to know you."

After a few further introductions between the two caretakers and the other residents, I turned to Gina, who was much shorter than me. She looked up and smiled, and I was immediately taken by her expressive dark eyes. "Gina, what beautiful dark chocolate eyes you have. You look so pretty. Did you know that?"

I was sure I could see them sparkle just that bit more as she soaked it all in. Then after a short pause she spoke. "Thank you, darling," she responded, with an expression of awe, wonder and surprise.

With her stocky stature dressed in a fawn tracksuit and her mop of thick dark hair, she had the appearance of a cuddly bear and her face showed she was a push over for compliments. I wondered how often she received them. I was privy to some of her files later on and it seemed compliments may have been rare. She attended primary school until her mid-teens but did not make friends, tending to be a loner. Gina may well have had learning difficulties that went unattended (which was nothing unusual in primary schools), and she drifted through those years without having any reading or writing skills. I could see her as a shy girl standing back from the other students in the school yard, alone and neglected. In some ways, she looked like that child — just thirty-something years older.

Gina remained living with her family — parents and several siblings — when she left school, then worked on and off in some clothing factory. Soon after leaving school she experienced her first psychotic episode, which resulted in years of intermittent visits to psychiatric wards. Everything went downhill from there and she had many life experiences living amongst strangers who tried to help her. Most of her family members did not abandon her, and the only reason their relationship became estranged was due to Gina's 'mental status', as she would become violent in their presence. They never gave up on her, but were most upset that she seemed to be getting worse as she grew older.

There she was, sitting before me in great anticipation of the yummy cake I had made for her visit. Everyone tucked in while I spoke to her two carers. I then showed Gina her room and the rest of the place. Thankfully, she and the other residents seemed relaxed and comfortable with each other and were happy to share in afternoon tea. After about an hour, with some flicking through magazines, Gina and her entourage left. She turned back to take another look. I could only guess what she was thinking but she seemed pleased. I was left to ponder why this dear lady presented so negatively on paper as she waved with one hand and held a magazine in the other.

The new week arrived and so did Gina with her two carers. For the first two days, I was able to observe how the carers interacted with her. They were most caring, attentive and supportive towards her. But I felt they were being manipulated by Gina, who simply learnt how to get what she wanted when she wanted. As I observed this, I felt she was in no way a demanding, nor dominant, type. She'd merely moved into the typical behaviour we may all learn from childhood.

In psychology, this is termed behaviourism, a form of conditioning to behave a certain way through life according to what our actions or words illicit. That is to say, when we automatically do something, we generate a specific outcome that will either bring about a reward or punishment for us. Logically if we get what we desire, we will repeat that behaviour for the desired consequence.

For example, if we do something that is perceived as positive we may receive praise or a treat, and conversely, if we do something negative, we may receive a scowl or worse. Naturally, some children test this process and see how far they can get, with a tantrum in a supermarket, for example. Well, Gina seemed to have found her forte for attention and these two carers — and most likely many others over the years — were her victims, as they literally jumped to attention the very instant Gina even looked like she wanted something.

The pattern was such that she would barely start a growl (which could turn into a loud pitch scream) and they would mobilise forces to offer Gina a cuppa, give her a shower, take her for a walk, etc. At times she just needed to look grumpy to get her way. They were constantly on full alert!

I didn't want to offend the carers by questioning their approach (after all, I did not know Gina's history with them at that stage), because clearly they had Gina's best interests at heart. However, I had seen enough so I made a suggestion and put forward a formal request to 'the powers that be'. I proposed that I didn't need the two carers for the whole twelve days and could we possibly shorten that to a quarter. I did push the line that one of the residents did not settle well with extra staff around — not a lie, actually — and I felt everyone would adjust sooner if we started the normal routine as soon as possible. I was most persuasive and then grateful to have that understood and accepted. Overall, the two extra staff members remained for four days total.

Then came the day the two carers left. I had previously explained to Gina that this house was her lovely home and was for all of the ladies, her new friends too. I told her they liked to have a nice quiet home to enjoy. I pointed out the 'quiet areas' (which was everywhere except her room), and she appeared to understand. I also reiterated if she felt like shouting or screaming, then she could do so in her room only. She agreed and so now, on this first day free from her carers, I again reminded her of the need to respect this rule.

All was well for a while, but by mid-morning only Gina was left, as the other ladies had gone to their day programs. Gina had not yet been able to attend any day programs and was only allowed in the community for a couple of hours — accompanied by two staff for support. I felt Gina was regretful when she saw the other ladies leave to attend their special places that morning. I did explain and even promise her that I would work at getting her the opportunities they had too. This was something she loved to hear as she kept asking if she really could do that. With her history, I felt it may be tricky but I was determined to find a way.

It was about 11am; Gina had finished her morning tea and had gone into her room to rest. But she soon returned and that was when the 'incident' happened. I had expected it and was ready. I happened to be writing up a report, with Gina standing about two metres from me. She began screaming in a high pitched shrill. I did not look up from my work. Her first scream was rather long, and after the second one, when she had to pause to draw breath, I stopped what I was doing and casually walked to her. "Gina, I said this is a quiet area, remember? So if you want to scream then do so in your room," I said in a very firm and definite tone.

After a brief look of shock, she stormed off to her room as I shouted out after her, "And close your door too!"

Well, she slammed it didn't she. *How dare I not rush to her attention like everyone else did?* she was surely thinking. She did keep up her 'song' for at least five minutes and it sounded very violent, but I felt unperturbed as I knew she needed this form of expression for some reason and it did no harm. From reading some of her history, I felt she had plenty to feel angry or frustrated about and, possibly, her form of psychosis was related to memories. I say this because over time Gina's verbal responses, idle chat and smiles told me she was enjoying her new environment.

But for now, Gina was going to learn she had to respect her new home and friends. After it was quiet again, I knocked on her door and entered her room, finding her sitting on her bed. She may have been reluctant to face me too. But I decided not to draw attention to what had transpired and simply put matters of her day into a friendly perspective. She didn't need more focus on the negative pattern of her previous years, as I felt sure she didn't feel good about it either. "Gina, it is lunch time soon so would you like to help me prepare a sandwich? You can show me what you like."

"Yes, darling," said she, sounding somewhat relieved as she daintily walked to the kitchen.

She learned with that one episode of screaming that she could not dominate or manipulate in her new home, but she was able to vent if she needed to without fear of punishment; if she felt like expressing her emotions that way, then she was perfectly free to do so any time in her room. There were a few times over the first few days when she forgot to go straight to her room but she took the reminders well and moved to her private space promptly — without slamming her door.

Over time, when she had this need to 'vent', it usually took the form of her standing in a corner of her room and looking directly into it while screaming with a high pitched shrill. In some ways she also seemed detached from it. One day I had to go up to the main office to do some photocopying. Gina had started her usual screaming, but I had to go and I needed her to come with me, as I couldn't leave her alone. I waited for her to draw breath. "Gina, I have to go do some office work, would you like to come help me please?"

"Yes, thank you, darling," she said in a sweet soft voice.

She hurriedly put her shoes on and walked with me calmly and politely, spoke in a friendly tone to others, waited patiently while I did some work and pressed the green button on the photocopier when requested, earning her lots of praise. All of this took about twenty minutes and then when we returned, Gina went straight back to her room, going into the corner to finish her screeching. I left her to it and carried on with my own business. Later she appeared from her room, asking when the other ladies would be back. This pattern continued and one time she awoke with scratches down each cheek. I asked what happened and she replied, "A pussy cat scratched me, darling, a pussy-pussy-pussy," as if she was a victim to such deeds.

"Well, you tell that naughty pussy to be friendlier or else it will have to go outside to sleep," I said.

I knew no such thing had happened, but I was sure she truly believed her version of events. It was clear this dear lady was very complex and her need to maintain her anti-psychotic regime was necessary, but she had vastly improved from the reports of her past. Prior to her arrival, her behaviour apparently had become so desperate that she was not able to visit her family, nor them to visit her. But after just a few months of living in her new surroundings, she enjoyed many happy visits and this was something that greatly surprised her family, so much so that one elderly relative was convinced she was cured of whatever her problem had been for over thirty years.

Also, quite significantly, for the next two years that I had Gina as my client, I never felt the need to administer even one PRN, let alone seek permission for the second. I have not in any way exaggerated any of this story, and I am so happy to report Gina presented as happy and contented with her new home and friends.

But the best was yet to come. As I indicated, Gina was aware of how the other two ladies were able to go out daily to their respective day programs, and she was wanting to do the same. I made it my personal quest to find a place for her. I had taken her out to places within the community from the first week — shopping, walking, the library and, of course, the 'cuppa-chino' with a cake — she was always a sweet lady and no issues ever arose. I also took her to numerous medical and specialist visits to busy clinics and large noisy hospitals, but she was an angel, responsive to my every request — naturally, I employed bribery to the fullest extent! I say this in jest, as to see Gina enjoy her treats in the canteen after her appointment was my treat also.

So there I was, phoning day programs. I had to conform to the dictates of her 'caseworker', and in this situation, a term I use lightly. I felt she was doing little for Gina since she had moved, and she resented that I suggested how I could do some searching to help her, as I often liaised with several day programs. I know she was a busy person, but her responses to me were short, cold and resentful. She even stopped returning my messages. How dare I intrude on her turf! I thought this field encouraged cooperation and not competition.

But I didn't give up on Gina, and I had time to build up my 'experiential report' by learning all the things Gina would be suitable for and, in particular, preferred engaging in. I eventually found a place that was perfect in every way for Gina. I spoke with the manager, learning about their programs and the general layout of the place. Naturally, I included Gina in this research, ensuring everyone was on the same page. It seemed the perfect place for Gina and I felt very happy for her. But, and this was a very big but, I had to formally go through Gina's caseworker. She was the one who had to agree and sign her formally to the placement. The problem was she never returned my calls. Eventually I caught her very early on the phone — she would not expect me to call at 7am — and told her about the placement I had found with much enthusiasm for Gina.

Well, this caseworker continued to be elusive and even reported me for interfering with her role. I was grateful for that because then I was able to draw formal attention to her relative neglect, her attitude towards me and how I had Gina's interests as my primary focus — not to mention what I had achieved with research, endless liaison and positive documentations, often in my own time. On Gina's behalf, I achieved my desired outcome and the naughty child in me was delighted to know that caseworker was forced to sign off on Gina attending my chosen day program venue. So with that, Gina started her one morning 'trial' — which we planned to gradually increase to five full days.

All this evidently meant a great deal for Gina as she proudly left for her first morning out. She chose her favourite track suit and looked pretty with her lovely dark chocolate eyes. We arrived at the day centre a bit after the usual morning scurry, and I introduced Gina to everyone: the supervisor, staff and Gina's prospective new friends. The place was buzzing, and I was feeling somewhat over-protective of Gina.

I wanted this to work for her as she had needed to do this so much. My plan was to lurk around the edges for the two hours that were planned as an initial introduction. But within half an hour, Gina did something totally unexpected — even above my usual positive anticipations. She must have been observing my watchfulness of proceedings. What she did next was so endearing. She placed both palms on my upper back, indicating the gentlest push forward and spoke quietly, "You can go now, Barbara. I'll be okay," in such a wise and sensitive way.

"Oh, of course, Gina. I was about to go soon anyway," I lied. "I will see you later on at lunch time."

After arranging a time to collect her, I left. And that was that — a resounding success in every way. Gina enjoyed her new confidence; she was proud to tell people of her daily deeds and I stopped my fussing. How was all this transformation so easy? Maybe partly due to how Gina felt about herself in a different environment. Maybe she decided her other ways of behaving were too hard to sustain and did not give her what she needed anyway. Maybe she liked herself more. Whatever the reason, I knew she was not going to regress as long as she was made to take responsibility for her behaviour and that she was liked for who she was, despite her many complexities.

This ritual of standing, staring and screaming into the corner was the expression of her psychosis, but I felt it was harmless and perhaps a kind of stress release against her confused status. Her day placement staff also gave her a designated area to perform this 'venting ritual'. It was still necessary to have her full daily psychiatric drug regime and her weekly anti-psychotic injection, and that was not my decision. My responsibility was to help her manage her life.

I shared this new more confident version of Gina with her psychiatrist during the quarterly visits. We did not know what potential hallucinations formed part of her psychosis, or what environmental cues may have triggered certain memories. Nor did we have access to those memories. We assumed given her relative standard of intellectual/cognitive capacity, it was such that she was unable to express her more complex thoughts. But I never debated her explanations of matters that seemed imaginary to her — such as those cat scratches. By not confusing her sensibilities, she was able to remain confident and that enabled her to reach her full potential.

EIGHTEEN

"See the person, not the disability"
— Unknown

This notion of changed behaviours in different environments reminds me of one client who used to attend my Outreach base. This was Connie, and each Wednesday morning her elderly parents, who were devoted to her care, would drop her off and collect her in the afternoon. For the four other days of the week, Connie attended a large centre for her day programs, and I knew it was busy and noisy there, so I suspect she responded more agreeably to our smaller group setting.

My plan was to keep this Outreach project going after the initial two years of helping settle those first five new clients. As many of the clients integrated into the larger day centres, the six other Outreach venues in and around Melbourne closed down. I saw the need for certain clients to engage in their daily activities away from a large crowd, so I petitioned to keep the Outreach program going — thankfully good sense prevailed. I believed the more intimate and quiet environment brought out the best in the clients who attended that venue.

Connie was just one example; she was middle aged and required some assistance with mobility and communication.

One day while helping her get lunch, I saw paper crumpled at the bottom of her bag. I took it out and found it was a letter from the large day centre Connie attended. It was addressed to her parents and requested their daughter pay for mugs she had broken — evidently the letter never made it to them. Curious about this breakage, I phoned the centre and the staff informed me Connie had been behaving violently over the past weeks, and this behaviour was escalating. I was astounded to know that as during those same weeks, she had presented in a completely different manner on her weekly Outreach day — not a hint of this 'other self'. To us, she appeared a sweet, patient and happy lady.

That told me a great deal about how certain environments can trigger different emotions, and something I have seen demonstrated repeatedly over many years. Perhaps we can all relate to how certain people or environmental cues might bring out the worst or best in us. We are all essentially the same, after all.

A recurring theme emerges throughout all our lives. It is as if we are all parts of a large life tapestry and we get to weave under and over, within and without, making beautiful or complex patterns; sometimes the threads get caught or even torn. Likewise, if we held a tapestry up to various lights, it may look quite different. Also it can relate to how the observer sees how the tapestry appears, according to their perspective. No two people make the exact same interpretation of any given piece of art. I can see how this theme translates significantly throughout my stories. The many complexities of each individual are even more perplexing when considering those who are on the autism spectrum.

From recent research, it has come to light that most of us can exhibit some autistic traits. I saw in a recent documentary on SBS how one professor who'd studied autism for fifty years declared she could identify at least three traits in herself, but these helped her with her ability to study. To be diagnosed as autistic, one needs to tick lots of trait boxes associated with the condition, such as preferring to retreat from others. Being able to focus or concentrate well is another character trait that is also notable. Being of high intelligence is another for some, and they may be brilliant at mathematics, for example.

However, these kinds of expressions can be fitted into the mainstream range of behaviours; it is only when a trait interferes with how an individual functions or develops that it is considered problematic. These days the term autism seems to have developed into a label that has become overused. I knew of one child who had a food allergy that caused him to behave erratically, and for a time he was considered 'autistic' by one doctor. Later when the allergy was discovered and addressed, the child's behaviour changed to within a normal range of expression. Yet the use of the label 'autistic' left its mark and two years later the parents continued looking for more signs of autistic behaviour with a degree of anxiety.

Autism still remains a puzzle as there are many variables, so these days the experts refer to someone as being along the 'autism spectrum'. Alarmingly, reports of this condition are on the rise globally, similar to reports of a rise in food allergies. These days special schools cater for children who are unable to cope in a mainstream school, and many of those children make positive advancements in their learning to cope in the world. Yet nearly thirty years ago, I had hardly heard of autism and when I found myself working with two young men who were diagnosed with it, I assumed it only had one form of expression, which closely resembled an ID person, even though I noted clear differences in each young man's personality.

I arranged for an educational session with an expert on such matters and the most I learned from that was of a few standard considerations. These were that autistic people need routine, may react to sudden changes, may get their emotional expression mixed up and don't cope well around crowds. I did not know about the vast range of individual differences, or even about Asperger's syndrome — the autistic status at the 'higher order' extreme end of the spectrum.

I did eventually see the movie *Rain Man*, which demonstrated another potential form of autism, regrettably known then as 'idiot savant' but now known simply as 'savant'. Yet I still felt I did not have a proper handle on what autism was all about, and cannot necessarily claim much more useful knowledge even today. I decided to focus on what my two clients were capable of and how I might promote that further. I tended to not buy into the fear of the unknown either, which led to me taking some risks.

It was coming up to Christmas in Melbourne, where we have what is known as the 'Myer's Window': an annual themed window display — extremely artistic and imaginative. That particular year, I read it was the best one ever with each window depicting a different children's storybook theme. While I had never been to see one of these pre-Christmas specials, I believed each window would depict a whole range of miniature colourful scenes — my two autistic clients seemed to enjoy focussing on such images. Just hearing about it set me on a mission that, quite frankly, horrified many.

Well, there I was, trying to convince management to let me take those two young men into the city by train, during the busiest time of the year. Back then I didn't fully appreciate how impossible that must have sounded. I genuinely could only see how much these men would enjoy it. I even felt this was going to be their once in a lifetime opportunity. I didn't have time to let the worry set in.

I felt it prudent to take another staff member along. Thankfully, my colleague Janine Cording accepted my request to assist us on our excursion; she was someone I completely trusted to be the perfect presence for such an undertaking. Janine has a beautiful heart and is naturally suited to working with the disabled, as she always sees her clients as people first, treating them with dignity and respect. I feel sure that having her on board helped get approval for my plan.

At that time, we were privileged to have Robin Whitchurch as our boss, someone who valued parents, staff and clients alike, which earned her much admiration and respect. So with those ladies' seal of approval, I was able to approach Jason and Sam, my autistic clients.

"Jason and Sam, guess what? Janine and I are going to take you on a lovely outing in the city. We are going by train to see very special Christmas storybook images in big windows, and then have a special lunch treat."

I was not expecting an answer in words as these two never spoke, but I felt sure they understood a great deal. Sam was in his mid-twenties and appeared a shy introspective person, who would never wander away from where he was meant to be. He always looked as if he could do with a good feed and a warm hug so I made sure I spoke to him often and engaged him casually. He was given lots of different experiences, and mostly flapped his hands a little when showing his pleasure. His smiles appropriately matched his experiences too, so I always felt I knew where he stood, emotionally.

Jason was a little younger, being in his early twenties. He arrived at the centre with the decree he was still an adolescent. In contrast to Sam, he presented as more emotionally volatile and needed to be watched carefully from absconding. Upon his arrival, he was assigned to my group and for several days he laid in a curled up fashion on a rug next to the group. I felt he needed time to adjust to his new daily environment so allowed him that until I knew it was time to encourage him to sit with us. Mind you, he always got up and came with me for his meal breaks and such, but that was as much as he could manage for a week or so.

Jason seemed to trust me and complied with requests. Unfortunately, he often seemed to confuse his emotions. At first it was difficult to watch how at times he would cry while shaking his hands violently and looking extremely anxious. I learned through experience that these reactions did not mean he was unhappy, as he would react this way sometimes when doing things I knew he liked, such as walking around the park. On the other hand, there were times when I knew he hated doing something, such as sitting with a noisy disruptive person, but he would laugh hysterically. This compulsive element of confusing his emotional reactions made for an unpredictable feature of his care. Nevertheless, knowing him and what triggered his behaviour gave me an edge to support him. It was interesting to observe how his form of autism found expression.

Back to our impending adventure. The two men remained calm as I explained what they may experience, including some yummy fast food they did not usually get. Jason gave me a quick glance in response, and Sam made a guttural sound that I took as approval.

My lovely co-worker Janine and I were hot to trot off to the city, armed with our two young men for a special outing. We all walked away that fine day in a happy relaxed state, leaving a stream of anxious energy behind. Hmm...

So there we were at the point of no return. Once on the train, we sat Sam and Jason at windows so they could watch the world go by. By the time we arrived at Flinders Street Station (an iconic landmark in Melbourne) the train was crowded with Christmas shoppers, and the station and street was like a colourful moving sardine can of people. We each looped arms with our client, who, standing casually beside us, waited in unperturbed fashion for the street lights to change as the trams rattled along. We walked along Swanston Street to Bourke Street, and still it didn't even occur to me to worry as we finally arrived at the Myers window site. Before us was a sea of people — the area crowded with far too many children for my liking.

After giving the other people plenty of time to see each window, we made our way politely through the human layers to view the windows ourselves. I had my camera ready and was impressed with how the two men focussed on the window display. Jason had his nose literally pressed to the glass and I could see his eyes focus on each wonderful fantasy storybook scene. Millions of little details, all life-like and set out with such artistic flair — I could see why this was reported to be the best annual display ever.

After a good length of time at each window, we moved them to the next. I took photos of each window and my two clients, their faces looking so intently at the scenes. Finally, I suggested we find a place for lunch and, again, the two men complied without fuss. The lunch area was crowded, but the fast food was immensely enjoyed and washed down with more junk. They evidently loved it!

We travelled back along the busy noisy streets to the equally crowded station, and thankfully did not have to wait long for our train. Once agreeably seated, we headed home. However, several stations on, Jason began to cry. His tears were plentiful, and his voice grew to a high pitch scream. I sensed he was offloading emotional energy and that he was otherwise fine. He may have even been sorry to be leaving. He did not try to run or move, but I sat directly in front of him as I held his hands firmly and kept reassuring him everything was alright.

Imagine how the other travellers felt. I assured them that he was fine and not to worry. Had they been scared, they could have easily moved to another carriage, but they remained. While Jason kept his scream up, Sam seemed relaxed and calm, just fiddling with his fingers. Looking back, it felt very surreal.

After over thirty minutes, the train arrived at our station. To my upbeat "here we are", Jason suddenly became quiet and casually stood, folded his arms and nonchalantly walked to the door as if he had just been woken. Then he strolled in this very relaxed casual fashion along the crowded platform to the exit.

I could sense the passengers' eyes as they watched Jason instantly transform in such an unbelievable way. I tip my hat to how those travellers remained and seemed to trust that all was well, despite appearances. I also hoped those people, and the ones at the hospital lift site with Jane, understood a bit more that just because someone appears threatening, the situation may not be as it seems. Mind you, I would never have blamed anyone if they'd left.

To this day I have never forgotten that experience, and I wonder if Jason and Sam have special memories of those storybook windows. I set up a special album full of the photos I took and Jason, in particular, peered at each photo as if he was there again.

For the rest of the day back at the centre, all seemed usual and the next day the men's home contacts reported nothing different about them.

So the question remains, how was it possible for us to achieve this experience? Was it by our subjective genuine beliefs that all would indeed be well that we changed the energy pattern against conventional wisdom? Perhaps the positive outcome was due to a kind of 'self-fulfilling prophecy' effect with any fear taken out of the equation? Perhaps, at a stretch, one might even suggest the young men knew we took a risk for them to enjoy a magical day so they responded accordingly.

NINETEEN

"If the world thinks you are not good enough... get a second opinion"
– Nick Vujicic

On the subject of forming positive expectations, I will relate one more story that required this approach. Roger was in his twenties and due to visit our centre with family and staff. I was informed that Roger had been 'vacated' from several other places due to his behaviour, and certain official individuals decided to trial our place. We were told that in order to make a decision as to his new placement, they would see how he responded to a given place to ensure they accepted the right placement offer. Hmm, that sounded complicated as I felt he may be running out of options. Although I had not expected to meet him during his visit that day, I inadvertently ran into the troupe. I had gone to the centre's workshop to deliver a message and on my way out Roger confronted me at the door.

My immediate reaction was based on the young man's expression, which told me he seemed anxious/nervous — understandable considering he was in a strange setting and had all this anticipatory attention on him. Perhaps he came prepared to let us know who was going to be in charge and took that defensive stance. But there he stood before me. He was my height and it looked as if his dark hair had battled with his comb. I did not even glance at his entourage as I was focussed on Roger and wanted him to feel at ease. In a sense, we were the only two people at that encounter, so I spoke to him directly.

"Oh, hello, you must be Roger. I heard you were coming to visit us today. I'm Barbara," I said as I put out my hand to shake his sweaty palm and weak grip — indicating he was indeed nervous. "Oh, I can see you would make a great worker here with those big hands, Roger, and I bet you will do a great job too — maybe even be our star worker!" I blurted the words out but he seemed to blush at the potential of that status. I sensed he knew he was perceived negatively, having been dismissed by several other facilities. With my positive banter, I offered him an alternative self-reflection — a chance for him to have a fresh start.

"Yeeh," he said coyly and with his huge grin.

With that, everyone laughed and Roger dropped his shoulders as the tension left his body. I had to rush on so we parted ways with me saying I would see him again soon. The next day I was informed Roger had chosen to join our centre, and that was the start of a long-term placement for him.

Proud but insecure was my assessment of him, and it is not unusual for someone like him to present a bravado and even a bullying stance as self-protection from their own projected sense of fear. Roger did learn the workshop skills well (simple packing of bolts). This was a functional/social activity with music and a large window to let sunshine in. For the rest of his week, he joined the various groups related to 'independent living skills', and made a whole new group of friends who accepted him comfortably — a case of the fearsome lion who became the pussy cat.

Roger never seemed to produce the 'old' behaviour that had earned him such a negative reputation of threatening others physically and verbally, as was reported by the previous centres. I felt it must have been very upsetting for his family to have gone through what was perhaps years of unwanted negative reports about their beloved son, and now finally he had settled to presenting as a proud young man. He was a lovely student and we spent much time together. While he did seem somewhat 'huffy' at times, he listened to reason to curb his emotions to an acceptable level. Thankfully, he discovered he could do things another way to produce different outcomes.

I've mentioned my Outreach service several times, which was witness to many wonderful memorable experiences. There is one that stands out as the most endearing of all, enabling two people to share some precious time with each other more than in any other setting. I am referring to Peter and Molly, who were clearly bonded in heart in every way, yet they rarely spoke words to each other.

The extent of their 'romance' consisted of little more than the occasional elbow nudge when sitting or standing close to each other. Their connection was evident even though no words of love were shared. It was never mentioned by those of us who were astute enough to notice, and it never went beyond that gentleness. However, there was one special day when their connection found expression in the form of a play.

Peter was a tall large-bodied man in his fifties, always groomed very neatly in conventional smart clothes. He presented as quiet and sensitive and did not speak other than when referring to his 'lady-love' as 'olady'. Molly, also in her mid-fifties, was short and stout in body, and wore 'sensible' comfortable clothes (a girl of my heart). She had little hair on her head and wore very thick glasses. She was gorgeous and beautiful in every way that counted. She could use words wisely but in a limited way.

"Olady," Peter would say with a nudge.

"Oh, Peter, that's rude," Molly would respond grumpily, with a cheeky smile to match Peter's.

That was just their way of communicating to each other, by way of endearment. They were our 'special couple' who seemed to revel in that one day per week when they could spend more quiet time together — sharing a walk, a café stop and some craft work. If one was absent, which rarely happened, the other was clearly disappointed so reassurance that the other would be back next time seemed appreciated.

Mind you, they did know each other for many years, attending the same large centre, but it is easy to become lost in the crowd or at least not have the same atmosphere where one could nurture one's thoughts and feelings. Molly could be who she wanted to be in this fairytale space. I assumed that one of her dreams was to have lovely hair as I noticed how she would search for images of women with nice hairstyles in magazines. There was a pile available to her at the Outreach base and she was very selective. I noticed she gravitated to the same selections when at the library too.

"Do you like how that lady looks, Molly?" I would ask casually as if only half interested, so as not to draw too much attention to what she was looking at. A very private person was our dear Molly. I was always keen to hear what she was thinking to give me clues about what she may value, looking for new ways to enhance her life.

"She looks nice," was something she usually responded with, but no follow up.

I questioned her this way several times with brunettes, blondes and redheads, but her most enthusiastic response was for a shoulder length light brown look. It was of an older looking lady, and I presumed that was what she could identify with. One day, after some formal investigation, I went a little further and asked, "So, Molly, how would you like to look like that? By wearing a wig? Maybe we could go get you one?"

"Yes, please," was her immediate answer, as if she had waited for ages to be asked just that.

Within a few weeks, after a flurry of agreements and approval for funds (the red tape ensured that any client's funds were accounted for in triplicate!), we found a suitable wig shop and made our way to the big city via train. I have little recollection of where it was located, or much else about the day except of being on the second floor of some very old room with wigs adorning the walls, and benches rested below a large mirror.

There Molly sat like some film star, trying on this and that wig. Lots of laughs at some and real stares with others, as if she couldn't believe what she was seeing in the mirror. Having finally selected one, we left with Molly being at least a head taller, I kid you not — and she hadn't even got the wig yet. She had to wait a few weeks for them to custom-make the wig, but in her mind I think she was already wearing it.

Given that Molly loved the concept of having new hair, I wondered about new clothes. She always wore garments that seemed drab, worn and too old for her age. I don't mean this as a value judgement, but we seemed to be on a roll with this modern update, so I asked her if she would like to buy new clothes.

"No, thank you," Molly replied politely with a smile. "I've got enough clothes."

So that was that. She was a lady of modest needs and knew exactly what she wanted.

She was delighted when her wig arrived. She even seemed to walk more confidently and tended to offer a bit of extra cheek to her beloved such as, "Oh too fat, Peter," nudging her bag gently into his hip area. This only gave him opportunity to call her an "olady" once more with giggles. Very cute.

Then one day, with her crowning glory in place, two things happened. The first was that someone donated new magazines, and the second was the news of Princess Diana's wedding. Now that sure got Molly's attention. Images of the royal wedding were in every possible magazine, and the one we had was nearly worn out — thanks to Molly. She seemed content to not take any magazine home for her own reasons, despite being offered. But noticing her interest in the wedding theme had me concocting a plan.

As the group joined in on a discussion about their favourite movies and TV shows we developed an idea of doing a play. This was part of our 'Social Studies' session, which led to ideas for some special projects. The intention was to stimulate the clients' imaginations and experience a bit of fantasy. On that particular day, each seemed interested in a program that was on the previous night — something on the royal wedding. Even those who did not have speech demonstrated their interest with their attention to my comments as I pointed to details on a page from a magazine. "Isn't that dress lovely with the beads all over it," I would say. "Hey, girls, look at this guy all dressed up. Does he look like a penguin or a spunk?" This was followed by much laughter — an emotion I always promoted whenever possible, as humour can be such a source of healing.

The art and craft sessions were much enjoyed by all, involving a variety of mediums such a glass, material, ceramic, pottery and paper. Likewise, making themed cards to give away and posters to adorn their rooms enabled them to express themselves more creatively, as well as enhance their skill sets. They may well have been simple by design, but quite complex when one's coordination or cognitive ability is compromised. With all this activity, the wedding theme evolved, and I knew I had Molly's full attention. "How about we do a Princess Diana/Prince Charles play, and we can pick out who will be the bride and groom?"

Silence... Everyone stopped what they were doing, almost in mid-air. I went on. "Maybe you, Molly, could be Diana and what about Peter being the groom?" I asked with boldness and hope.

To my delight, Molly was quick to respond. "But I haven't even got a wedding dress."

"That's no problem. I still have mine," I said, having thought that through already. "I can bring it in for you to wear and can get a special necktie for you, Peter, as you are always already dressed as a spunk!"

Seemed like us girls had railroaded the prospective groom into just going along with the plan. To be honest though, apart from blushing somewhat, Peter just kept silent. But he was extra cheeky about calling Molly 'olady' and nudging her on a short walk later that day, which told me he was not opposed to being assigned to the role.

We prepared for the play to go ahead the following week, so the usual 'guests' would be present. We also discussed how we could make a special cake, play music and get flowers.

"Just like a real wedding," said Molly, who had fully embraced the idea.

When the big day arrived, I helped Molly into my wedding dress — plus the veil — and I don't think she moved for at least five minutes. She just stood there, looking at herself in the bathroom mirror. Naturally, I took a photo of her, but not with Peter in case someone misconstrued it. I gave Molly a copy of her photo but she declined to take it away from the Outreach base, which informed me that she was reluctant to reveal her secret outside our influence. I concluded that at least she could carry some lovely memories.

As for Peter, he played the handsome prince charming well, nudging his 'bride' down the aisle — expressing his standard declaration of love. As touching as it was, I doubt the other wedding guests noticed much more than the appearance of the event, but they did enjoy the wedding party, especially the part when the cake got distributed amongst them.

The following week, no one mentioned this affair. However, every now and then Molly would take the photo out of a drawer to look at herself in the wedding dress. She did not discuss this and the other clients seemed not to notice, but perhaps they simply understood her need to remain private with her thoughts. However, from time to time they did comment on her nice hair, to which she responded with a large smile. Thankfully, Molly always seemed to be content and satisfied with her lot overall. Perhaps she found her greatest joy in her mind, as I often caught her smiling alone.

With the 'wedding play' over, this group moved on to a

different focus. First up, the military band was set to perform their monthly free concert at a local venue open to the public. The following month was to be a visit to a Morning Melodies event at a local hotel. There were lots of 'cultural interest' opportunities to attend, but it took organisation. Staffing and transport were always an issue, but the numerous concessions and the special 'companion cards' for the staff made access to certain venues possible. While I was not involved in sport, other staff enjoyed taking their clients to the footy, and that was such a wonderful opportunity for the eager fans. Thus, it was always on with the show!

TWENTY

"The most beautiful things in the world cannot be seen or even touched, they must be felt straight from the heart"
— Helen Keller

There was a time when I supported some of my clients with a fortnightly social community event run by a local church. Essentially, anyone could attend for a simple catch up, to listen to music or engage in a variety of craft activities. This experience also provided a way to surreptitiously offer some counselling when more worrying personal issues arose. The atmosphere was relaxed and the room décor provided a warm friendly atmosphere.

Caring and sensitive volunteers helped run this service, which mainly regulars attended. All seemed to have health issues and some form of disability. I could well understand why people were attracted to this place, as everyone was treated equally. It seemed apparent that most of the participants were very independent individuals and, within this setting, they could feel perfectly normal and capable in all the ways important to them.

I was especially taken by a young woman, Katie, who was transported to and from this venue via taxi. She made an attractive picture, with her slim shapely figure, pretty face and mid-length wavy, dark hair. She was blind, her hearing was greatly compromised and her speech limited. However, despite having a loving family who could support her, she preferred to live alone, managing her small unit and daily activities. No disability was going to stop her and she genuinely appeared content. I am sure she felt pleased with herself in being able to achieve her lifestyle to that degree of independence, which alone would ensure she felt personally satisfied. I believe she had friends who visited and that she was house-proud. She wore colour-coded clothes: she developed a label system that indicated by shape/touch the colour of a clothing item.

I admired her attitude on so many levels. And her spirit reminded me of Helen Keller, who was also blind and deaf. I presume Helen Keller is well-known to readers here but if not, I heartily invite you to look her history up, as you will be astounded by the way she focussed on her 'abilities' and moved forward in her long life proudly. Hers is a fascinating story. Born in 1880, Helen lived to eighty-seven. Prior to contracting a disease as a toddler, she was an early talker (from age six months, I read), so evidently very intelligent. But she lost her two most important senses, her sight and hearing, never to regain them. As a consequence, she became wild and unruly over those early years and was allowed to eat her meals by grabbing food from anyone's plate while they were sitting at the table, such was the parents' pity of their 'poor little girl'.

By the time Helen was a teenager, she became more unmanageable and even a danger to a new baby in the family. In exasperation, her parents employed a tutor to help and, against great odds and significant determination, she was able to teach Helen to spell out words using a hand/

fingering system termed the manual alphabet — part of the sign language deaf people use today. Helen later went on to use braille as well. Over the years, she went to college, became an author, a political activist and travelled the world. According to her biography, she wrote to and met twelve U.S. presidents. Helen believed we must all use the potential of our own minds. A movie, simply called *The Helen Keller Story*, was made about how she presented as a child and how she changed. It is a remarkable story and one movie well worth viewing.

Back at the church-run community social day, there was Frank, in his mid-forties. He was a proud man who took great care in his appearance. He walked cautiously due to a faulty hip, but it did not stop him catching public transport to shops, church and to this community outlet for his friendship base.

Frank also lived independently so enjoyed contact with others. He liked to chat but he had difficulty conveying his thoughts, so patience was required. Nevertheless, he was quiet and unobtrusive as well as helpful in ensuring others had their biscuits with their cuppa — he became a much-loved member of the group. He was keen on his artistic endeavours too, and one day he said he would like to make me a picture but didn't know what to paint. I suggested he paint how he felt about his life. That idea seemed to please him enormously.

Several weeks later, he proudly presented me with his lovely creation and could hardly contain his excitement as I opened the package to discover how he perceived his life. Despite his various disabilities, he focussed on his abilities and evidently things looked good to him. There were a few fluffy white clouds floating in the intense blue sky, over lush green grass and a range of colourful flowers on tall stems. The whole image was dominated by a large smiley sun with its bright yellow wavy beams of light bathing the landscape below. I looked at Frank, who was matching the huge smile he drew on that sun. I knew he was keenly anticipating my response.

"Wow, and wow," I said to him, telling him I was so pleased he saw his life so positively and thanked him profusely for sharing it with me.

It happened to be a grey rainy day when he gave me the painting so I also said he is someone who can still see the sun shining just above the clouds, even on a grey day. I had been informed about Frank's earlier years, when he had not been in a good place, so I was very grateful this 'sunshine man', as I referred to him, had broken away from the negatives in his life to find peace and joy. He gravitated to people at the social group and this opportunity to express himself in a way that enabled him to feel good about himself.

Against the backdrop of demonstrating simple kindness, I have seen how the opposite can be if experiencing a disharmonious environment. Having an abusive, threatening, controlling and nasty style towards clients is only going to perpetuate more mistrust, fear and even violence. Erratic behaviour can be a symptom of this disharmony and mistrust. There is a need to be informed and 'read' a given situation. If ever in doubt, seek support and guidance. Of course, this works for us all. For Frank to experience the best in others meant he could experience another way of living his life more positively.

There are children born every day who will be diagnosed with some congenital or genetic disorder that renders them disabled. However, there are those who present with 'learning disorders' that may be managed in ways that make a huge difference to their futures. Fortunately for Helen Keller, her parents were able to pay for a special tutor to see how their beloved daughter could learn. She was essentially provided with the opportunities that enabled her to not only thrive but flourish, despite her deaf and blind status. We don't know how many children's talents were/are being lost to our society due to relative neglect and, in particular, poverty, thus denying them their full potential. But our own prejudices about disability might be one of the most harmful things that keep a child from reaching their full potential. We may even stifle their progress by our loving default of expecting or settling on so much less from them. It is a delicate balance, however.

I was once given a book called *The Woman Who Changed Her Brain* by Barbara Arrowsmith Young, who was born in 1951 and began life with a severe learning disability. Her book describes her clinical mysteries and triumphant outcomes. She related how her research helped her understand her problem and, with this knowledge and newly developed method, she opened a school in Toronto in 1978. Now, her self-taught method of the cognitive training program is being implemented in schools in Canada and across the United States.

Barbara Arrowsmith Young explains how she was able to overcome her struggles as a child all through her years of schooling, and how 'handicapped' she was over those years. Her quest is to help others find a way to override their brain function issues and to teach her method in order to help many other children worldwide who struggle with similar 'learning difficulties'.

If you think this story does not seem possible — that she couldn't have been that 'handicapped' — then I challenge you to get a copy of her book. It might just help a child you know who is currently presenting with learning difficulties. She is yet another person who refused to accept how others place limiting expectations on those with a disability, by not believing there is always hope and potential for anyone to grow. Young was never diagnosed with ID and she managed to struggle through her formative years by coping with school work through extra diligence and exhausting effort, but no one was really aware of her true capacity until she became an adult and explored her potential. That's the point. Fortunately, she had the ability and presence of mind to explore more herself.

I have an 'ideal' notion for anyone who has some free time each week and feels some affinity with the disabled. There are too many children with various difficulties to overcome who may do well with special one-on-one attention. Volunteering is serious business but can be hugely rewarding for many reasons. Activities can include reading a book with a child, visiting a playground, going to an animal refuge where they can pet kittens or take puppies for a walk (even if by wheelchair) — the list is endless.

As loving as parents can be, many may already be overloaded with other children, or simply with life's difficulties and not able to manage such experiences with any kind of 'quality', let alone quantity. A small respite can do wonders for the child and the family. We must never judge as we cannot know how others are feeling in their unique circumstance. I would even suggest that not even a parent with a disabled child can fully know how the experience feels for another parent in the same situation. We all have different coping mechanisms, supports systems, emotional tendencies, and strengths and weaknesses for dealing with life.

There are numerous groups that cater for the disabled, and special schools for their education and guidance, which would be readily forthcoming for volunteer work, even within the school or home environment. All community centres would have contacts for such places within any local area. Naturally, for volunteer work there are strict guidelines about who is eligible, which includes formal requirements such as a police and working with children check to offer greater security to the disabled. I am sure the need for some child to have that special attention is significant. I am reminded of that saying of how it takes a whole village to raise a child. It is something we overlook when we have our own concerns to focus on, but perhaps volunteering can even reduce them.

Even just a small variation to one's experience is worthy of the effort. Once I was working near a facility where a five year old girl named Minna lived. She always wore a pretty dress and her thick black hair framed her delicate coffee-coloured features. She looked like an expensive porcelain doll. This delicate little beauty happened to be blind and deaf. One day while walking past some rooms, I noticed how she was lying on her back on a rug. She was not in danger but she could not move her body and I wondered if her world experience may have matched this position of, well, flatness.

While there were other children there — she could not see or hear them — I wondered how aware she was of anyone in her world. Those days, I did not really think about how we can pick up the energy of others around us, be they negative or positive, but now I assume she was fully aware of not being entirely alone. She may at least have felt the vibrations in the floor as people moved about. But back then, I thought it a good idea to ask if I could give her a light massage.

I stroked her hands and arms, tried to move her limbs and placed her on a bean bag so she was in a more supported position. I recall someone walking by and asking me why I did that and I replied so she could see out the window. I was asked if I knew she was blind. To which I replied her being in that position might generate different stimulus — perhaps some light. I felt rather silly for having said that, but looking back I think I got it partially right. I especially hope the extra movement and touch was a positive experience for little Minna and gave meaning to her. I say this with regard to Helen Keller's overriding philosophy in her quote at the start of this chapter: "The most beautiful things in the world cannot be seen or even touched, they must be felt straight from the heart."

I was grateful to learn later how such things as touch can offer a positive sensory benefit to those like Minna. Also, how sensory deficits can be overridden by other parts of the brain, as people who are blind report 'seeing' their world, even with colours. Likewise, touch and massage can generate different sets of stimuli that enhance one's health by providing numerous benefits. Even the notion of hugging is thought to enhance one's sense of wellbeing.

But these days the term 'personal space' can be a contentious issue for varied reasons. From the early days in the field of disability, I read that as a professional, one must instruct a client to keep their distance and not allow them to hug staff, and staff were not even allowed to refer to clients with endearing names such as sweetie or darling. Now it is unacceptable for staff to touch a client unless absolutely necessary and if they do, they must first gain permission. This comes under the sexual harassment umbrella, and is not something to be taken lightly.

I completely understand the need to respect all individuals, and the need to never take liberties or to assume that our clients can be approached in any way other than professionally. But taken to extremes, this can sometimes create a dilemma. Over the years, I have found there are clients who may approach someone and spontaneously reach out to give them a hug. Likewise, there are those who don't have family and the closest thing they have to feeling that 'loving connection' is with their regular staff.

So with all our cautionary approaches these days, new policies to protect clients have been developed. We now operate under an atmosphere of suspicion. I am aware of how the 'bad apple' staff of the past have generated mistrust and caused policy to change over time. For example, once it was discovered client's funds were open to theft, with some carers helping themselves, a strict code of handling client's funds was introduced — one that involved lots of paperwork! It was a case of abusing trust. Likewise, when some carers were found to have physically taken advantage of their clients via abuse and neglect, guidelines were introduced that outlined appropriate behaviour such as proximity of space and limited touching. In order to protect our clients, it means that, unfortunately, in some situations, we may have thrown out the baby with the bathwater.

TWENTY-ONE

"The biggest disability of a person in life is a bad and negative attitude"
- Anurag Prakash Ray

While the majority of my interactions with the disabled have been delightful, there have been a fair share of frustrations too. At times, if feeling overtired or overloaded, I could catch myself sounding somewhat fractious — which is not acceptable at all. Thankfully, I kept my best 'patient' self for my clients, and hopefully my family didn't feel they got the short end of the stick on that count! But then, I must extend kindness to myself by remembering the wise words of Alexander Pope: "To err is human, to forgive divine."

Over the years, I have also experienced a degree of exasperation towards other staff with certain approaches to difficulties, at a time when complacency can lead to negative outcomes. Cooperation between all staff is the key to ensuring a harmonious environment. It is all too easy for certain personality types to show a superior stance over those who are less able to assert themselves. ID clients can make easy targets, especially if they are unable to talk. Thankfully, a strict reporting system is now set in place to protect clients from negative elements to their care.

Nevertheless, vigilance is required at all times so that only staff with integrity are employed to care for the disabled. Likewise, the compatibility of all participants between staff and clients needs close attention as everyone deserves the right to feel safe in their environment. That includes the need to appreciate how clients interact with each other. If certain work environments become too difficult or if a level of unpredictability arises from some issue, appropriate advice and support is woven into the support system of which each worker is a valued part. If it is needed, seek that support.

However, fearing the unknown when facing potential challenges means you may miss an important opportunity to help your client find a more positive way to interact with their environment and others. Emotions such as frustration, anxiety, confusion or even physical pain can be behind a client's violent outburst. We can look for cues to help those clients understand why they may be feeling upset, rather than turn away. Staff support is always at hand. It also pays to remember the message I mentioned previously: that all too easily a culture of violence is often perpetuated in the presence of fear.

Please know that there is no weakness in asking for help; it actually demonstrates strength. But if you feel that your best strategy is to request a transfer, then that needs to be considered rationally. There is nothing to be gained from trying to be a superhero or ignoring such personal insights. The aim is for a win-win solution in any given situation.

You need to feel on top of your game when dealing with your clients, not weakened by uncertainty. Your tone and actions will blow your cover anyway, so explore your strong areas by extending kindness to yourself too. That way, you will be the most effective in helping your clients find their own strengths. There are many ways to help each individual feel a sense of empowerment. It is up to you to take a stand for them and yourself.

I spent years studying psychology but will never fully understand the many complexities of this thing called the 'human condition'. I do know this much for certain: if you feel a sense of superiority over your clients, then they will feel subservient to you and that will either lower their self-esteem or lead them to mistrust you and become defensive with negative behaviours. The truth is that not one of us is better than the other, despite there being many unique differences between us. Our clients don't need our pity; they need to be treated as equal. Everyone deserves a chance to feel they are equal for every one of the reasons that are important to us all.

By being a disability worker or carer, you can hold the key to offering the opportunities and appropriate experiences for any person to feel good about themselves, regardless of their disability level. Likewise, when you support them out in any community setting, you can feel proud of how you are helping raise awareness of the need to help others embrace all differences amongst us. In the human services field, there is no room for those who need a role to express their sense of superiority or dominance. As a worker, you are there to help show your clients the way. If you aim to do that, you know you are working with complete integrity.

Today in Australia, a disability worker requires a Certificate IV in Disability; this is to ensure that current policy and professional standards are met. In the mid-eighties, staff were required to participate in an abundance of training. It seemed that no funds were spared to ensure staff were operating as professionals. Special 'networking' days were organised so staff from a wide range of facilities around Melbourne could come together and share ideas and support. Sumptuous free lunches were part of that deal. It was impressive. But then it ended.

These days, the Department of Health and Human Services Victoria also provide extra training as standard. They include the required mandatory certificates in first aid, fire safety, medication administration and a variety of specialised areas related to functional requirements and management of various forms of disability. I feel certain that if staff were motivated enough to lobby the managers of any facility for the disabled to get a specialist to instruct them about issues related to their clients' needs, then that would be arranged.

I believe good people work in the policy area and are keen to promote the wellbeing of both staff and client. We need to feel less like it is 'them or us' and function collaboratively. If staff don't want to be treated as robots, then they must not behave like them. I remember once when a new initiative was introduced in a certain facility in the form of a monthly prize to be awarded to the most valued staff member. I rejected that notion outright, as I saw the imperative of that work environment being a cooperative one, and not competitive. The idea felt antagonistic to fostering positive team work.

Knowing there are changes afoot with the evolving NDIS initiatives now and over the next few years, it is necessary that staff are considered as credible members of the system of care to the disabled on all levels.

A few years ago at a meeting, some participants, who came from a range of different professional occupations, shared that their desire to change jobs was due to "wanting to make a difference". Overall, it has been my experience that if someone is open to the needs of others, they are appropriate to their important and valuable role in working with the disabled.

Never underestimate that being on the front line makes you very valuable for helping promote your clients' wellbeing. Consider it a privilege to be there for them. Not because you may think they are needy, but because through your quality of service you can make a real difference to them. Just because someone is labelled ID and may not be able to speak or move well, does not mean they unaware of how you perceive them. Your role comes with many benefits beyond your pay cheque, as through your sense of humility, you can learn more about yourself.

Once, I even learned from an imaginary encounter with a disabled person. It was 6am on a cold dark wet winter's morning, and I had been up until 2am completing an assignment. I awoke cursing my alarm in a grumbling mumbling self-pitying mood. I climbed out of bed and suddenly swung back around, staring at the spot I had been lying. There, I visualised a quadriplegic looking at me, talking to me in no uncertain manner: "Oh, stop complaining! I would give anything to be in your place. Let's change places."

It completely stopped me in my tracks and forced me to change my thought direction, and although this happened over twenty years ago, I still think of that 'experience' often. That memory has helped me confront busy days working with my clients with a good measure of pleasantness and appreciation, regardless of how tired I might have been.

Remember, it can be that first greeting you give your client that sets the tone for their whole day, so please appreciate the quality of your presence. If earning money is the only motivation for working in the disability field, then you may fall short of your true potential. There are so many more valid reason for you to be there.

I feel gratified how our dear Robbie managed to find his way to enjoy his ABBA music. So often his facial expression — deeply focussed and involved — gave me the impression he was truly transported to where he was free to fly to great heights. Sometimes I would catch a certain smile as if he held a special secret. It was a delight to see his joy. Music was his forte, and it can never be overstated how many ways are available to ensure each of your clients feels a sense of empowerment. If you help them explore all possibilities, then you will truly make a difference to the lives of others.

TWENTY-TWO

"Fairest and best adorned is she
whose clothing is humility"
– James Montgomery

I once had a special friend who was left disabled by polio as a baby. Jean was already elderly when I came in contact with her, just as I was learning about disability. She was the first person I ever spoke to who was most in tune with the concept of humility. Jean knew how it felt to experience a mobility restricting form of disability, but her determination and inner resolve ensured she focussed on the positive elements in her environment and used them to help her enjoy her life as much as possible.

When someone hurt her, she focussed on the considerate people in her life. A kind word here, or a thoughtful deed there. When it was cold and wet and she felt isolated in her tiny flat, she looked out the window and watched how wondrous nature was, even if it was just the beauty and form of one small tree against a backdrop of grey — the rain on the sill became small silvery jewels. She felt warmth in the company of her little Billy the budgie, and when it was time for him to go, she had her little soft toy friends to talk to. With limited funds throughout her life, and in a constant state of discomfort with her leg irons, Jean exuded an attitude of gratitude and shared this with others until the day she departed.

I first came across Jean while working as a volunteer in Canberra, where I visited the homebound. One of the people I met was a ninety-four year old lady, who lived alone with her two cats. She shared her concern that she was no longer able to write to her dear friend Jean, who lived in another state, so she asked if I would write on her behalf. That was the start of several years of correspondence with Jean, whom I sadly never met in person. I could tell from her letters she had much wisdom from her wonderful philosophical approach to life, for despite all the many hardships she'd endured over the years, she could still see the beauty of life and believed in the goodness of people.

Jean told me through our correspondence that she and her siblings were dispersed to various foster homes as young children, and she never learnt where they went. Because of her polio, she spent much of her childhood in and out of hospital, and this was interspersed with foster home placements. She felt none of those relationships gave her comfort or showed her any kind love. Once, she even tried to conceal a special doll she had fashioned out of a wooden peg, with a pencilled face and a small piece of cloth tied around it for a dress. One of her foster 'mothers' discovered it, snatched it away, then burnt it. She was heartbroken about the loss of her 'friend', and had no one in the world to share her sorrow with.

Years passed by without anyone visiting her in hospital, and with no one to focus any special attention on her. She craved to have just one friend. When she was a young woman she met a wealthy man who befriended her. From memory, I believe they met in a park. She may have taken this as true love but when his family found out he was fraternising with a poor 'cripple' lady, they made him leave her. He was evidently weak or merely using her because he gave in to his family's request.

Jean was pregnant with his chid at the time, but this made no difference to him. She just wanted to be loved and belong to someone who cared. Her baby son filled that void. Jean was unable to work so she had to depend on charities to help her find a home and some scant furniture. She was given a commission flat on the second floor of an apartment block along with a meagre array of objects needed for basic living. Jean was appreciative of any place to call home and determined to raise her son with love. She said she never felt like a victim.

It was difficult to manage alone with a child as her leg irons made it painful to walk. She needed to wear them to support her legs, as the polio had left them undeveloped. Imagine having to carry a baby and groceries up and down stairs for years. Ever so poor, Jean was devoted to her child and was at least able to show him the love she always craved. She said she felt sorry she could never afford to buy him a little bike, which he always wanted, but she could at least sit and share books with him.

Her son grew up and married, and had two daughters — and a motorbike. Sadly, he and his small family moved away for work. This meant visits were rare. Jean enjoyed her son's letters and photos and never complained. However, I could tell she was lonely, but also happy to know her 'family' was getting on with their lives as best they could. She possessed a forgiving heart and her love was unconditional.

Jean wrote about her surroundings, which seemed rather

drab. Yet in her descriptions, she did not focus on the old brick wall, but the tree branches in view near it. She marvelled at how the leaves changed to beautiful colours and how she loved seeing the little birds build their nest in the tree each spring. If it rained or was frosty, her focus was on the silvery shine that edged the window sill or ground; on a clear day she wondered at the patch of blue sky.

Her special friend Billy was a cheeky little budgie, and from all accounts, learned to talk well. He was able to fly around freely in her dwelling — such was their special relationship. Billy would shed the odd feather and Jean collected them. One day she sent me a beautiful floral design made out of Billy's feathers. She carefully glued the tiny soft pale green feathers onto a black velvet cloth neatly pressed into a small gold photo frame. It is one of my most precious possessions.

Even though she did not admit how desperately poor and alone she was, it was only to my many written questions that I knew her personal story. She was matter-of-fact about her disappointments. I truly believed she did not define herself by her lack, but by what she had — she made the most of that in every possible positive way. She was a grateful and appreciative person and an inspiration to me. Jean was always open to telling her life story with a sense of wisdom and insight. I think she enjoyed being able to talk about all the things that, perhaps, needed to be said.

One time Jean shared a story — just another hurt she had to endure. While still in her middle years, she saw a newspaper article talking about a prominent person whom she recognised as one of her brothers. After much ado, and cautious excitement, she made contact with him and he invited her to attend a social event he was hosting in his opulent home, which was about an hour away.

That rainy evening, Jean was left to get herself there via taxi, feeling both excitement and trepidation as to how she might be received. It was a devastating experience. Upon her arrival, she was left standing amongst the finery of everyone else's outfits, in her drab clothes and leg irons; she heard whispers about that "cripple" in a negative tone. Her brother did not introduce her to anyone and largely ignored her, so she quietly retreated out of there, returning to her lonely flat. She never heard from her brother again.

"It just wasn't meant to be," said she, as if his behaviour was excusable. Yet she spoke with compassion, suggesting he may simply have been too weakly influenced by others. This experience made her close the door on ever trying to find her other siblings.

One day Jean discovered she was going blind. She still found some positives in that, saying how she would be able to imagine beauty based on her memories, and how we could still share our monthly 'chat' via a cassette recording. By then her beloved Billy-bird had passed away, so she held on to some special soft toy animals for comfort and love. Her favourite was Omar the camel. Once I heard her voice quiver when she told me how she'd allowed a disabled child to take him home. The little girl had been visiting with her mother and had become attached to Omar, crying when she had to put him back, so Jean gave it to her. At least she still had her ceramic doll Belinda, which looked like Cinderella at the ball!

Jean relied on volunteer help for her daily hygiene and meal requirements, which also provided limited socialising. In previous years, she had a weekly shopping outing and an occasional lunch or café treat, but eventually, Jean only managed the strength to attend medical appointments. Still, I never heard her complain and she had lots to share on each forty-five minute cassette she sent me. The closest time that dear lady ever came to mentioning anything of her 'lack' was when she spoke of how she missed being free to roam along the beach and how she dreamed of one day being there: "I want to be wiggling and twisting my bare toes in warm soft sand in sunshine."

Knowing she was dying, Jean spoke of genuinely looking forward to being free from her shackles, and on one fine day I received a letter informing me of her departure. Holding it in my hands, with eyes closed, I saw her in my mind's eye: she was smiling, overlooking a beautiful beach with sunshine spread over the clear turquoise water and soft golden sand, upon which Jean left her special 'squiggly' footprints.

While still with her sight, Jean was motivated to write something inspirational to the disabled. I now introduce you to Jean in the form her special offering.

HUMILITY

I knew I was beautiful, I had seen myself reflected in the gentle flowing river that had passed by my roots for at least half a century. A tree that had given shelter to little feathered friends, listened to their young twittering to each other. It was a very peaceful and lovely life, even though I had been through many storms, and threats of bushfires. Looking back, I think I could have even been smug, so contented was I in my bush setting. It is so easy to feel that way when there is nothing to really bother your serenity. Why, just being a tree was enough reason to live. If only we could live the way we thought was best, but somehow things do not always work out the way we want.

I'll pass over the next period of my experience, as it is far too painful to contemplate, even thinking of it my sap runs cold. I was chopped down, and without dignity, I was hauled away to a saw mill. Why? Well, I might be made into a beautiful polished table, and in vision I could see candles reflected on my surface, a vase of flowers adding beauty to happy conversations and fine food. Of this I was sure, as I would not be cut down without reason. With these thoughts in mind, I felt a little better. So much for dreams! When I finally left the horrible, dreaded mills, there I was stacked with the rest of me. In ugly slats. SLATS! What could anyone do with these useless things I had become: once a tree of great beauty, reduced to this. I soon lost all interest in my welfare, for I was now nothing.

I was taken to a factory, along with the rest of me, and left to the whims of mankind. I was battered, belted, and then put into intense heat to be bent more easily, and to be seasoned. Some evil smelling substance was painted over me, and then I was 'finished'. But what had I become? I certainly was not a thing of beauty. I did not resemble anything I had ever seen before. Suddenly I heard a voice saying, "These are beautiful crutches, just about the best we have made." I was a 'CRUTCH', but what was that, and who would want me and what would be my use? It did not take me long to find out, as I was taken (and the rest of me) to a hospital. There

I spotted many others like me, and when I saw the work they had to do, a great change came over me, for I knew I would be wanted and needed very much by somebody.

My 'somebody' turned out to be a beautiful young lady, who would need my care and protection for the rest of her life. She hated me at first — resented my necessity. As we worked tirelessly together each day, respect grew between us. I was thrilled to feel the tension leaving her grip as she learnt to leave most of the work to my 'twin' and me. She trusted us, we were the very first things she reached for, and I feel proud to say we never let her down. For years we lived through laughter, tears and all her experiences. Envy and regret were forgotten as devotion took over.

After almost twenty years of service, my 'twin' suddenly broke. Oh, the heartbreak over that experience! We then had to be replaced by aluminium 'things', which my special somebody dislikes even to this day. I now stand alone in a corner of her bedroom. Sometimes she runs her hand over me and says, "You are never forgotten, my faithful friend, for these new-fangled 'things' are not in your class. I cannot depend on them as I could on you and your 'twin'. These clatter and fall where you never did. Dream you dreams, but be assured you did what you were designed to do, and no one could do it better."

Jean Rogers — Written in Sydney for the Foundation for the Disabled on 4 March 1986.

Inspirational Acknowledgements

I dedicated this book to a lady who personifies the true meaning of *compassion* and *love*, because our world needs so much more of this energy that flows from heart to heart.

Moira Theresa Kelly A.O. is a multi-award-winning Australian who was born in 1964. She has been described as a humanitarian worker and global peacemaker. She is so much more. Moira is best known for bringing Bangladeshi conjoined twins, Trishna and Krishna, to Australia for life-saving surgery. They are now thriving in her care. She is also well-known for her ability to solicit support from hospitals, surgeons and health staff for seriously ill children in need of complex medical attention.

As a young woman, Moira worked in many Third World countries in orphanages and places of poverty, including a time with Mother Theresa, who became her inspiration at the age of eight after seeing a missionary film about her work with the poor. Moira has devoted her life to charity work by helping sick and needy children, and their families, from around the world. Thanks to Moira's efforts, many have made a transition from an experience of significant disability to renewed hope for their future. Towards this,

Moira established the Children's First Foundation, located in Melbourne, Australia.

A current project is the Global Garden of Peace; a non-political and non-religious Australian charity Moira founded in 2013. Moira's inspiration for this came while on a medical rescue mission to Gaza, Palestine.

To Moira's quest of making the world a better place she adds "that gardens and playgrounds are the centre on which to build a community around a respect of children's right to play." I invite you to watch Moira's special YouTube video: Global Gardens of Peace. The amount of planning going into it will astound you.

We are all living in the same world that needs healing from much hurt, misunderstanding, confused directions and uncertain destinations. Thank goodness for those individuals who help shine a light on our path. I would like to highlight a few who speak to us all across the ages:

- ❖ *Our prime purpose in this life is to help others... If you can't help them, at least don't hurt them* — Dalai Lama (on Compassion)

- ❖ *Be kind to all creatures; this is the true religion* — Buddha

- ❖ *Let the one among you who is without sin be the first to cast a stone* — Jesus Christ

- ❖ *The greatness of a nation and its moral progress can be judged by the way its citizens and animals are treated* — Mahatma Gandhi

- *Let us realize the arc of the moral universe is long but it bends toward justice for all* — Martin Luther King

- *A loving heart is the truest wisdom* — Charles Dickens

- *In matters of truth and justice, there is no difference... Issues concerning the treatment of people are all the same* — Albert Einstein

Another remarkable person I would like to acknowledge is Pam Ahern, a champion for justice and kindness. She stands up for those sentient beings who are starved, neglected, diseased, disabled and abandoned, then are finally shown how love feels. Founder of Edgar's Mission, a not-for-profit sanctuary for rescued animals in Victoria that seeks to create a humane and just world for humans and non-humans. She named her mission after her first rescued animal, Edgar Allan Pig. Pam's motto: "If we could live happy and healthy lives without harming others, why wouldn't we?"

Another worthy person is Lyn White, Campaign Director of Animals Australia (www.animalsaustralia), who works tirelessly investigating animal cruelty. Her quest is to "Leave the world a kinder place".

Lyn, along with Moira and Pam, deserve your ongoing admiration and support.

VOLUNTEERS

Last, but by no means least, there are those who find many ways to help uplift, heal and support others. I think this quote best sums up these unsung heroes: "Volunteers are not paid, not because they are worthless, but because they are priceless" — Unknown. They must be valued as some of our best 'national treasures'. Volunteers are the ones who ensure charities, foundations and hope funds thrive. Their driving force is compassion and their fuel is love. These individuals are found in all walks of life and in every community.

Take, for example, Gwen Barratt who, along with her husband George, is there when someone needs support from their burdens, with one hand on her heart and the other in her pocket. Just one of many examples of her thoughtful work is the annual box of beautiful garments Gwen knits for children in Third World orphanages; her effort and kindness is exemplary of her attitude to help make the world a better place.

Another special person is Patricia Farnell. Despite her own financial hardships and health difficulties, Pattie has spent many years growing thousands of beautiful plants to sell at local markets with the proceeds going towards animal rescue shelters — animals who need support seem to find her wherever she goes.

It is gratifying to know how our youth have embraced the spirit of kindness. Someone who demonstrates this dramatically is Rachel Chalada, who received the 'Life Saver of the Year Award' from the Darwin Surf Lifesaving Club when she was a teenager. She became the youngest member on the Northern Territory Search and Rescue Team (SAR), qualified as a lifeguard and won gold for an event at the Surf Lifesaving/Royal Lifesaving Championships in Sydney. She was described as "a very bright star" in *NT Surfline*, 21 January 2010. Due to her community contributions, Rachel was awarded 'Darwin's Young Citizen of the Year' at age seventeen.

Along with the many other 'stars' who uplift us in numerous ways, we each only need to do simple things to help generate change so that our disabled citizens can feel more supported, understood, valued and enabled to be positively integrated within our society. All it may take is for some of us to be able to re-think our attitudes and perhaps modify our behaviour towards those who need our support most.

I sincerely appreciate you taking the time to share this journey down memory lane with me as well as the individuals who have found their voice through their stories. They only ask that we observe this golden rule: to never see anyone as less important or less relevant than ourselves. If we remember that and have an open mind with all interactions, we will make a difference.... especially to the 'Rainbow People'.

About the Author

Barbara grew up in a semi-rural township on the outskirts of Melbourne. Her early school years were disrupted so she continued her studies from age thirty. From that time, her welfare officer connections opened the door to her involvement with the disabled, but once she completed her Bachelor of Behavioural Science studies, she qualified to start her practice in psychotherapy.

Over time, Barbara sensed her true calling was with the disabled, as she felt this direction provided her with the most rewarding work experiences. After a couple of years of juggling between the two career paths, she felt challenged to make a choice and has never regretted that her heart won.

With encouragement from her daughter in recent years to write about her experiences, Barbara realised this avenue provides an opportunity to share her insights into the lives of the disabled, as a means to helping others understand them better. By sharing their stories, and with the intention of helping dispel many misconceptions of what it means to be disabled, she offers them a voice, enabling them to tell you who they really are.

www.ingramcontent.com/pod-product-compliance
Lightning Source LLC
Chambersburg PA
CBHW031504270326
41930CB00006B/249

9780987617712